The

Outrage

of

Amoral Sex Education

ES Williams

The Outrage of Amoral Sex Education
is published by Belmont House Publishing

First published September 2006

ISBN 0 9548493 0 2

Published by Belmont House Publishing
36 The Crescent
Belmont
SUTTON
Surrey SM2 6BJ

Website www.belmonthouse.co.uk

A Catalogue record for this book is available from the British Library.

Printed by The Cromwell Press
Aintree Avenue, White Horse Business Park
Trowbridge

Cover Image from: *4Girls: A Below-the-Bra guide to the female body* published by the Family Planning Association

Contents

Sincere thanks to Patricia Redmond
for her help and encouragement in completing this book.

Preface

In my 10 years as a Director of Public Health I saw sex education at first hand. At the heart of sex education was the claim that condoms protect young people against both pregnancy and sexually transmitted diseases. Yet as an experienced public health professional it was clear to me that the evidence did not support this claim. Moreover, as a Christian I became increasingly alarmed by the explicit nature of the literature that was being distributed by various health promotion departments to persuade children to accept the Government's 'safer sex' message.

While official policy is that parents should be consulted over the sex education of their children, the reality has always been that the details of what is taught is kept away from parents. This means that in practice parents have little idea about what actually happens in sex lessons, and most are content to leave their children in the hands of those who claim to be experts in the field of sex and relationships.

But there is growing concern that all is not right in the land of sex education. Frequent newspaper horror stories mean that more and more parents are starting to feel uneasy. The purpose of this short book is to bring parents and grandparents, as well as teachers and church leaders, face to face with the reality of sex education. My mission is to shine a light on the sex education industry. My hope is that those reading this book will be in a better position to decide what they should do to protect children from the worst excesses of state-sponsored sex education.

1

A shameful record

It is now widely accepted that there is a crisis in sexual health among teenagers in the UK. It is often quoted that we have the highest rate of teenage pregnancies in Western Europe. According to Prime Minister Mr Tony Blair we cannot afford to ignore this shameful record. Every year some 90 thousand teenagers in England become pregnant, the vast majority of whom are unmarried. Around 8 thousand of these unwanted pregnancies occur in girls aged 15 or younger.

A parliamentary select committee has identified what it called an unprecedented crisis in sexual health. According to Professor Michael Adler, a key adviser to the Government on sexual health, 'It is no exaggeration that we now face a public health crisis in relation to sexual health.' All the common sexually transmitted diseases (STDs) have more than doubled in the last decade, the greatest rises having occurred among young people, leading to an explosion in the workload of genito-urinary clinics. The situation is so serious that the Government is setting up a national screening programme for chlamydia (a disease which may cause infertility) among young women. There are now almost weekly headlines illustrating the shocking nature of the crisis. The recent furore over a 14-year-old schoolgirl who was given an abortion, behind her mother's back, on the advice of a sexual health advisor from the local National Health Service Trust, has astounded, even shocked the nation. And behind the headlines are real young people; it is our children and grandchildren who are the victims of the crisis in sexual health.

Outrage over sex lessons in school

What is so disturbing about the crisis is that it follows three decades of intensive nationwide sex education. Respective British Governments have made sex education a major priority, claiming that it is the answer to the problems of teenage pregnancies and sexually transmitted diseases among young people. Yet the evidence before our eyes shows that sex education has not achieved the promised benefits.

An increasing number of people are starting to question the value of sex education. A report in the *Daily Telegraph* under the headline 'Outrage over explicit sex lessons', describes how parents are kept in the dark about the content of sex lessons in the school classroom. The *Telegraph's* education correspondent, John Clare, reveals that 12-year-olds are being taught about anal, oral and digital sex. 'Parents and grandparents wrote in droves to say how horrified, appalled, disgusted and outraged they were. Almost without exception, they demanded to know where the lesson materials had originated, who had authorised them and how widely they were being used.'[1] The article reached three conclusions. The first is that the use of crude and explicit sex education materials is widespread. Second, parents are not told the details of what is being taught and, third, parents have little hope of discovering what their children are taught.

Writing in *The Sunday Times* Cardinal Keith O'Brien referred to the draft sex education strategy of the Scottish Executive as 'state-sponsored sexual abuse of children'. The draft strategy, published in 2004, proposed sex education for pre-school children as young as three and four, dismissed abstinence and emphasised the need for greater access to contraception and abortion for schoolchildren without parents' knowledge or consent. According to the Cardinal, the Scottish Executive was putting unlimited resources into sinister sex education projects. Scotland was facing one of its biggest moral challenges in a generation. While the problems of high teenage pregnancy rates, increasing abortion and the explosion in sexually transmitted diseases are well known, 'less well known are the growing army of sexual health service providers who push a value-free agenda, focus on a biological/mechanical approach to sex education, treat children as adults, offer confidential access to powerful drugs and procure abortions for children without their parents' knowledge. This is all done at the expense of the taxpayer with seemingly limitless funding from the Scottish Executive for this failed agenda.'[2]

Cardinal O'Brien identified what he called a chilling agenda that amounted to little more than the sexualisation of children as the health and education services drive forward plans to contracept a generation of young Scots. He said that parents were appalled at the idea of young children being provided with graphic and intimate sexual instruction and predicted that many, determined to preserve their children's innocence, would revolt against Scottish plans for yet more sex education.

A study presented at the Royal Economic Society's annual conference resulted in a headline in *The Times* – 'Free pills and condoms "boost promiscuity".'[3] According to research carried out by Professor David Paton of Nottingham University, sexually transmitted diseases have risen fastest in those areas where the Government's policy on preventing teenage pregnancy has been most actively pursued. This is because expanding contraceptive services and providing the morning-after pill free to teenagers has encouraged sexual activity. The conclusion is that the increase in STDs among young people represents a failure of the Government's sex education policy.

Melanie Phillips under the headline 'The Trojan horse of sex education', describes the Government's sex education policy as a disaster. 'The increase in sexual promiscuity among children and teenagers is not due to ignorance but to the deliberate destruction of the notion of respectability. Not only are official blind eyes turned to enforcing the legal age of consent, but sex education actually targets under-age children. Moral guidance is nowhere.' The article mentions the wildly inappropriate sex education materials used in some schools. 'One such video shown to 9 and 10-year-olds enlightens them about different positions for heterosexual, bisexual, gay and lesbian sex. Other programmes require children to act out sexual behaviour. Such material looks like propaganda for sexual licence; some is so exploitative it verges on the predatory. Is it surprising that more and more children are acting out sexual behaviour, a common response to sexual abuse?'[4]

Sex education policy

Government policy on sex education is outlined in two documents. The first is the *Teenage Pregnancy* report (1999), prepared by the

Government's Social Exclusion Unit, which argues that the high teenage pregnancy rate in the UK is due to ignorance. We are told that 'young people lack accurate knowledge about contraception, sexually transmitted diseases, what to expect in relationships…' The report concludes that there has been a drift into the serious error of moralising.[5] 'Whether the Government likes it or not, young people decide what they're going to do about sex and contraception. Keeping them in the dark or preaching at them makes it less likely they'll make the right decision.'[6] In the Government's mind any attempt to introduce a moral dimension into the discussion on sexual behaviour and contraception is not only unhelpful, but potentially harmful.

The second document is *Sex and Relationship Guidance* (2000), issued to all schools and health authorities. It explains that teaching schoolchildren about contraception is at the heart of the Government's strategy to reduce teenage pregnancy. 'Knowledge of the different types of contraception, and of access to, and availability of contraception is a major part of the Government's strategy to reduce teenage pregnancy.' It follows that 'trained staff in secondary schools should be able to give young people full information about different types of contraception, including emergency contraception and their effectiveness… Trained teachers can also give pupils – individually and as a class – additional information and guidance on where they can obtain confidential advice, counselling and, where necessary, treatment.'[7] They should also be provided 'with information about different types of contraception, safe sex and how they can access local sources of further advice and treatment'.[8] (Treatment is a euphemism for supplying contraceptives.) This means that children are to be given instruction in using contraception, and emergency contraception, and teachers can give children confidential advice about where to obtain contraception. According to the guidance, 'young people need to know not just what safer sex is and why it is important but also how to negotiate it with a partner'.[9] The ability to negotiate 'safer sex' is an important skill that sex education hopes to impart to schoolchildren.

Another aim of sex education is to help children to overcome their natural embarrassment and talk about sex. 'It is essential that schools

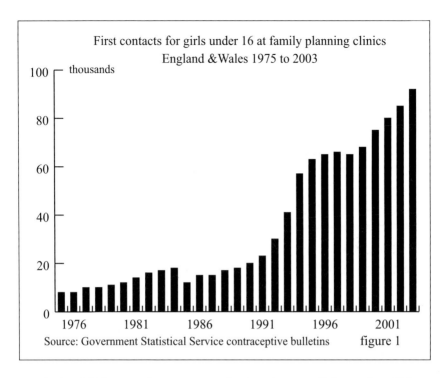

First contacts for girls under 16 at family planning clinics
England &Wales 1975 to 2003

Source: Government Statistical Service contraceptive bulletins   figure 1

can help children and young people develop confidence in talking, listening and thinking about sex and relationships. Teachers and other staff may need to overcome their own anxieties and embarrassment to do this effectively.'[10] The expectation is that schools will provide an environment where children feel comfortable discussing sex and contraception.

Contraceptives for children

The Labour Government's policy to increase the use of contraception among children must be seen in the context of current patterns of use. In the mid-1970s, as sex education was taking off, around 8 thousand under-16s were recruited into using contraception per year; by 2003 the figure had risen to 92 thousand – an elevenfold increase in 25 years (figure 1). Despite these alarming statistics, the Government is doing all in its power to increase still further the use of contraceptives among children. How many more under-age children does the Government want to visit family planning clinics? The shocking truth is that over the last three decades successive British Governments have succeeded in developing a contraceptive culture among children.

Emergency contraception became available in the 1980s. By the mid-1990s almost 800 thousand prescriptions per year were being issued. In 2003 family planning clinics issued 27 thousand prescriptions to girls under 16, and 77 thousand to young women aged 16 to 19.[11] The number obtaining prescriptions from GPs is not known. Yet the Government now has a major campaign to increase the use of emergency contraception among teenagers – even setting up a scheme in supermarkets to make it more easily available. A Department of Health spokeswoman said, 'We strongly support the involvement of Sainsbury's, working in partnership with the local NHS, to improve young women's access to free emergency contraception.'[12]

In the mind of the Government the crisis in sexual health among young people is simply that the promotion of contraception has not been vigorous enough, that sex education messages have not been explicit enough and have not started at an early enough age. So after three decades of sex education we are asked to believe the Government's assertion that the underlying problem is that young people lack accurate knowledge about contraception. We are asked to place our trust in the Government's sex education policy. The Government has set a target to reduce teenage pregnancies by 50 per cent by the year 2010.

Endnotes

1 *Daily Telegraph*, 23 November 2005, Outrage over explicit sex lessons, John Clare

2 *The Sunday Times*, 29 August 2004, Failing our children, Cardinal Keith O'Brien

3 *The Times*, 29 August 2004, Free pills and condoms 'boost promiscuity', Alexandra Frean

4 *Daily Mail*, 5 December 2005, The Trojan horse of sex education, Melanie Phillips

5 *Teenage Pregnancy*, HMSO, London, June 1999, p7

6 Ibid. p90

7 *Sex and Relationship Education Guidance*, DfEE, July 2000, p15

8 Ibid. p10

9 Ibid. p18

10 Ibid. p22

11 *NHS Contraceptive Services, England: 2003-04*, bulletin 2004/17, Department of Health, ed. Lesz Lancucki, September 2004

12 *Ananova News* website, 22 August 2002, Government supports Sainsbury's pill move

2

A brief history of sex education in the UK

So how have we arrived at the present situation where tens of thousands of under-age children are regular clients at family planning clinics? For the past thousand years biblical morality has been the foundation for sexual conduct in this country, and biblical virtues have been widely accepted as the only sure guide to sexual behaviour. How is it possible that Great Britain, once a great Christian nation, has fallen so low that the government is now issuing contraception to children in supermarkets?

The saga of sex education really starts in the early 1960s when the Family Planning Association (FPA) recommended the promotion of a parliamentary bill to provide for free advice on family planning under the National Health Service (NHS).[1] In 1966 the Minister of Health, Mr Kenneth Robinson, was invited to give the keynote speech at the FPA national conference. He said that planned parenthood promoted happiness and that lack of planning, often due to ignorance of effective methods of contraception, might lead to misery, ill-health and, in some cases, to criminal abortion.

The first Brook clinic offering contraceptive advice for young single people opened in London in 1964. Since then Brook has specialised in providing contraceptives for children under the legal age of consent, without informing their parents or GPs, should the child request that his or her visit be kept secret. The Brook manifesto *Safe Sex for Teenagers* (1978) made it clear that the underlying philosophy for staff appointments is that the customer is always right. 'We must be prepared to challenge our established attitudes that sexual activity in young people is dangerous... There are still too many workers in birth control clinics who believe, consciously or subconsciously, that sex before sixteen is sinful.'[2]

The demand for more sex education

After the introduction of the abortion act in 1968, there was widespread concern about the high number of abortions among young people. Although there were now over a thousand FPA contraceptive clinics around the country, David Steel, the main sponsor of the 1967 Abortion Act, claimed that there was growing evidence that the demand for abortion is caused by lack of provision for family planning. In 1970 the chairman of the Health Education Council, Lady Alma Birk, made an impassioned plea for more sex education for young people. She argued that contraception should be provided by the NHS, and suggested that to do so might save money for other social services.[3]

In the 1970s the Schools Broadcasting Council of the BBC beamed a series of sex education programmes to schools across the nation. These powerful visual programmes, delivered with the full authority of the BBC, set the tone for sex education in the UK. The explicit nature of the *Merry-go-round* series of films was highly controversial at the time. The third in the series was obsessively preoccupied with the sex organs, including full frontal nudity. It shows small boys standing naked at the edge of a swimming bath, before the camera zooms onto the genitals already perfectly obvious in the distant shot. Another scene shows a male model posing naked, while the commentator makes reference to his pubic hair and penis.[4] A mother expressed her anger at the explicitness of the films. 'What concerns me is this: why, why, why the need for *visual* sex education? The children are shown a man's penis, and then its erection diagrammatically; today watching the particularly messy birth, we were then shown (again unnecessarily) a long clear shot of the mother's stretched and swollen pubis. After this, is it such a big step to saying "We have been so very frank up to a point, lest anyone still be in any doubt or ignorance at all, shouldn't we be totally frank and show coitus…" '[5]

The FPA acknowledged that most of the religious, medical and political barriers against which it had struggled for years had been overcome. 'Concern over the great demand for abortion has focused attention on contraception as part of preventive medical care. Many of the FPA's former opponents, spurred on by debates over abortion and pollution, now agree on the need for a massive extension of contraception services. The

Association is now allowed to advertise on television, and the Government has publicly stated that the provision of birth control is a priority task. Two new FPA clinics open each week, and the Association has well over 600,000 patients... the once remote possibility of freely available birth control services within the NHS now seems almost inevitable.'[6]

The *Longford Report* (1972), which examined the growing menace of pornography in the UK, concluded that the visual sexual images shown to schoolchildren were pornographic in nature. In the field of sex education, 'as many witnesses testified, the risk that the material may take a pornographic form or seem pornographic in the eyes of children, must be very great. In this respect the increasing visual presentation of sex education material becomes a dangerous tyranny. Parents may hesitate to withdraw their children from classes for fear these children will be ridiculed and isolated.'[7] This was a shocking indictment of the growing sex education industry. The unthinkable had occurred – images that would once have been called lewd and obscene were being used to 'educate' British school-children. Sex education, with the connivance of the BBC, had succeeded in legitimising pornography.

Free contraception for children

A report of the Royal College of Obstetricians and Gynaecologists, published in 1972, recommended 'that a comprehensive contraceptive service should be established in the NHS'.[8] A government review of family planning services concluded that a substantial expansion was needed to reduce the number of unwanted teenage pregnancies. The British Medical Journal claimed that a policy of free contraception would help cut the number of unintended pregnancies.

In 1973, around a Bill to reorganise the NHS, the issue of contraception for children was fiercely debated, with strong views expressed on both sides of the argument. Lord Avebury argued that an efficient and comprehensive family planning service would reduce abortion figures. He said that the 'increasing figures of abortion are evidence of the failure of the contraceptive services in this country. If you have a free and comprehensive family planning service, and you do not attempt to deny it to girls below the age of 16, then you will begin to get somewhere.'[9]

And so in 1974, by an Act of Parliament, the British Government became responsible for supplying contraceptives to children. It also took over the running of contraceptive clinics from the FPA. It was now Government policy for the state to provide contraceptives to children under the age of sexual consent. Henceforth, a child of 14 or 15, or for that matter even as young as 11 or 12, could go to a NHS clinic, drop-in centre or youth club to receive his or her free supply of contraceptives. This Act of Parliament represented a massive change in social policy and was a landmark decision in favour of the sexual revolution. And this major change in social policy, that was to have an enormous influence on the sexual mores of the British people over future decades, occurred without the general population really being aware of what was happening.

4Girls (FPA)

And the most disturbing aspect of the Act was that it allowed doctors to prescribe contraceptives to children without the knowledge or consent of their parents – and hardly anybody outside the family planning lobby was aware of this fact. Few people realised that doctors now had the right to prescribe contraceptives for children and keep the fact secret from their parents. So contraceptives have been freely available to under-age children on the NHS since 1974, and a number of ideologically motivated organisations, such as the FPA, the Health Education Council, later to become the Health Education Authority (HEA), and the Brook Advisory Centres (Brook) have spent millions of pounds of public money on promoting contraception among under-age children and young people.

FPA targets to reduce unwanted pregnancies and abortion

During the 1970s the FPA and the Health Education Council became widely accepted as 'sex experts'. Their mission was to educate the nation's children about sex and contraception. In 1976 the FPA announced targets to reduce by half the number of unwanted pregnancies and by half the annual number of abortions over the next 10 years. These targets, the

FPA claimed, would be met by improving sex education and the provision of contraceptive services.[10] In 1977 the Family Planning Information Service, sponsored by the Government, was set up to provide information about the availability of free contraceptives. Within two years the information service had distributed 12 million leaflets to GPs, clinics, educational establishments and health promotion officers. In addition, the service provided information for 150 radio broadcasts and 60 national TV programmes. Numerous articles were written for publication in various magazines and newspapers.[11] The country was, without any doubt, being flooded with sex education material. The resource list prepared by the Health Education Council was 23 pages long, including lists of reports, books, pamphlets and leaflets, posters and charts, films and filmstrips, slides, film loops and audiotapes, all providing information and resources for sex educators.

In 1986 the FPA reported that its information service had distributed over 50 million items of literature in the past 10 years. But the FPA did not mention its targets, launched with great fanfare in 1976, to reduce the number of abortions and illegitimate births within the decade. So how successful was the FPA in achieving its abortion target? The number of abortions in England and Wales increased from 130 thousand in 1976 to 172 thousand in 1986, a 32 per cent increase. And illegitimate births among teenagers more than doubled – from 19.6 thousand in 1976 to 39.6 thousand a decade later. Clearly, the FPA had not achieved its targets. What had the 50 million items of literature achieved? Had FPA literature actually contributed to the increase in teenage pregnancies? Why was an organisation that was receiving large amounts of public money not held to account?

The 'safer sex' campaign

In response to the AIDS threat the Government launched a nationwide 'safe sex' condom campaign in 1986-87. A television advert, *AIDS – Don't Die of Ignorance*, used an iceberg to propagate the idea that AIDS was a major public health threat. AIDS was now firmly on the political agenda. The slogan 'Anyone can get AIDS' was a powerful propaganda weapon in the hands of those who were intent on promoting a condom culture under the guise of 'safer sex'.

In February 1992 the Secretary of State for Education and Science, Mr Kenneth Clarke, laid before parliament a statutory order for a revised national curriculum for science which made it compulsory for 11 to 14-year-olds to be taught about HIV/AIDS and 'safer sex'. A booklet, *HIV and AIDS: a guide for the Education Service* was sent to all schools. It explained that HIV could be caught through drug misuse and infected blood products and through risky sexual activities. Teachers were instructed to avoid giving the impression that the disease was confined to high-risk groups such as homosexual men.[12] The guide described casual sex, multiple sexual partners, sexual experimentation and various unusual sexual practices in explicit detail. In a debate in the Lords, the Earl of Liverpool asked whether 11-year-olds were ready for such compulsory and explicit education, and Baroness Phillips asked whether the Government seriously wanted to defend a pamphlet 'which explicitly describes oral sex, which cannot be of any assistance in the subject, and may be totally misunderstood'. Lord Elton pointed out that the information was being put forward in an amoral context.

The Education Act of 1993 made it clear that 'sex education must be provided in such a manner as to encourage young people to have regard to moral considerations and the value of family life'.[13] It became a legal requirement for state schools to provide sex education, including information on HIV/AIDS and other sexually transmitted diseases, from September 1994. In primary schools the basic biology of sex was to be covered in science in the national curriculum. Any further sex education was optional, and it was up to school governors to decide whether or not to provide any more. If they decided to provide more sex education, 'they must publish a written policy on the content and organisation of the sex education, including information about the right of withdrawal'. Middle schools deemed to be secondary were legally required to provide sex education for all pupils and to publish a policy. There were no legal requirements regarding independent schools.

Even more contraceptive education

In 1996 the FPA was awarded a three-year contract by the Department of Health to provide a contraceptive education service. The chairman,

Dr David Robertson, thanked the Department for their consistent and unfailing support for the work of the FPA.[14] The service would supply a comprehensive range of leaflets on all the different methods of contraception and had a dedicated helpline for the public and health professionals. The FPA had already run a six-month campaign to improve knowledge about emergency contraception, including adverts in the national press, women's magazines and on radio. Information packs were sent to all primary health care teams, family planning clinics and pharmacists. The booklets *Is Everybody Doing It?* and *4Boys: A Below-the-Belt guide to the male body*, aimed at 13 to 17-year-olds, were launched. The booklet *4Girls*, published in 1997, was reviewed in *The Observer*: 'It is full of naked women and explicit descriptions of the female body. Pubic hair, breasts and masturbation are discussed in detail. But, if it is successful, a copy will be owned by every young girl in the country.'[15]

From January 2001, as a result of a Ministerial Order, emergency contraception was made available over the counter from a pharmacist for women aged 16 and over. Clearly, the Government's intention is to increase still further the use of emergency contraception among young people in the hope that it will help meet their teenage pregnancy target.

The first national strategy for sexual health and HIV, published in July 2001, aims to foster a culture of positive sexual health by making sure that everyone gets the information they need – without stigma, fear or embarrassment – so that they can make informed decisions to prevent sexually transmitted diseases.[16] Improving abortion services is a key aspect of the strategy. 'NHS funded abortion should be more readily available, ensuring that women who meet the

Is Everybody Doing It? – cover (FPA)

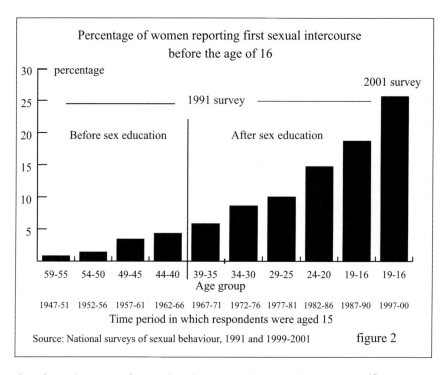

Percentage of women reporting first sexual intercourse before the age of 16

Source: National surveys of sexual behaviour, 1991 and 1999-2001

figure 2

legal requirements for an abortion are referred without delay.'[17] An extra £47.5 million was invested to support the new strategy.

In February 2003 the Health Development Agency published a toolkit, *Effective Sexual Health Promotion*, for Primary Care Trusts and others working in the field of sexual health promotion. Under the pretext of providing an evidence base for what works in preventing teenage pregnancy, the toolkit claims that there is a consensus that 'school-based sex education, particularly when linked to contraceptive services, can delay sexual activity and reduce pregnancy rates'.[18] This is a remarkable claim for the evidence shows that there has been a large increase in sexual activity among young people that coincides with the growth of the sex education industry, and no reduction in teenage pregnancy rates. In the 1950s, before the advent of sex education, it was rare for women to be sexually active before the age of 16. By the late 1990s, after three decades of sex education, around 25 per cent of women report first intercourse before the age of 16 (figure 2). In other words, the sex education era has been characterised by an increase in teenage sexual activity, and many people believe that sex education has contributed to this increase. It seems obvious that if we teach children about 'safer sex' and how to negotiate it with a partner, encourage them to think and talk about sex and provide them with free contraception, that some will be tempted into practising what they have been taught.

In 2005 the Government's Independent Advisory Group on sexual health, on which the FPA and Brook are well represented, recommended that sex education should be made a statutory foundation subject at all key stages within the National Curriculum, thereby guaranteeing every child's right to high quality, comprehensive sex education throughout primary and secondary school.

Endnotes

1 *The Times*, 25 October 1963, Birth-control advice by NHS urged

2 *Safe Sex for Teenagers*, Brook Advisory Centres, 1978, p23, p24, p27

3 *The Times*, 25 June 1970, Call for sex teaching

4 Mary Whitehouse, *Whatever Happened to Sex*? Hodder and Stoughton, 1978, p57

5 Ibid. p60

6 Family Planning Association, Annual Report 1969–70, p3

7 *Pornography: The Longford Report*, Coronet Books, Hodder Paperbacks, London, 1972, p232

8 Report of the Working Party of the Royal College of Obstetricians and Gynaecologists, *Unplanned Pregnancy*, February 1972, London, p91

9 Hansard. Lords debate, 12 February 1973, c 1338

10 Family Planning Association, Annual Report 1975–76, p8

11 Family Planning Association, Annual Report 1978–79, p1

12 *Daily Telegraph*, 26 April 1992, Patten faces challenge on AIDS lessons, Fran Abrams

13 Department of Education, Education Act 1993: *Sex Education in Schools*, circular no. 5/94

14 Family Planning Association, Annual Report 1995–96, p1

15 *The Observer*, 7 December 1997, Martin Wroe, cited from Family Planning Association, Annual Report 1996–97, p3

16 Department of Health, *The national strategy for sexual health and HIV*, July 2001, p12

17 Ibid. p28

18 Department of Health, *Effective Sexual Health Promotion*, February 2003, p16

3

The ideology of sex education

It is important to understand that the main organisation involved in sex education is the National Health Service (NHS). However, it is the Family Planning Association (FPA) and Brook Advisory Centres that drive the agenda and produce most of the sex education literature used by the NHS. Health authorities, and now Primary Care Trusts, with the assistance of the FPA and Brook, have been actively engaged in distributing this literature, some of which is used in sex lessons in schools.

Some of these materials are deeply offensive. In 1994 there was a furore when the Health Education Authority (HEA), a government quango, published its sex education booklet, *Your Pocket Guide to Sex*, which showed an angel astride a condom on the cover. The booklet, written by the agony aunt for *Just 17* (a salacious teenage magazine) contained information on the use of vibrators, oral sex and masturbation. In parliament Lord Stallard said he believed that the booklet promoted promiscuity and was insulting to women. The Earl of Lauderdale called it 'a glossy but degrading incitement to anti-family behaviour'.[1]

Valerie Riches of Family and Youth Concern wrote, 'Since it was established in 1968 the Health Education Authority has been surrounded by controversy over its approach to sexual matters. The "smutty" sex handbook for youngsters is just another example of its explicit and amoral liberalism. Last month the Authority, in association with a glossy magazine, *Company*, published 20 pages of completely uncensored facts, "69 Bravest Sex Questions: Bold, spicy, frank – they're the ones you've always wanted to ask". Readers were treated to an orgy of information about every orifice of the human body which the Authority deems suitable for sexual pleasure, provided, of course, that pregnancy does not result. Government departments have previously responded to public concern about the Authority's activities with evasion and prevarication. The Authority itself, which exists on public money, has hidden under the cloak of respectability of being an agent of the Government.'[2]

The Government was clearly embarrassed by the booklet and the Minister of Health, Brian Mawhinney, said that he found it distasteful, inappropriate and smutty and advised that the 12 thousand copies be withdrawn and pulped. The Health Education Authority responded that the booklet contained passages on celibacy and saying 'no' to sex, sexually transmitted diseases and contraception – information which would help to curb HIV and reduce teenage pregnancies.[3] The director of the FPA defended the booklet as one attempt to fill a gap, and a spokesman for Brook said the controversy showed that people did not understand the truth about sex education, and quoted the number of teenage pregnancies that occurred each year.[4] This controversy is important for it shows that even the most explicit, amoral sex education material usually contains a section on saying 'no' to sex.

To understand the ideology behind sex education we need to examine its literature. Because of the secrecy that surrounds much of what children are being taught, few parents see the booklets, pamphlets, leaflets and videos used to propagate the messages of 'safer sex'.

Promoting promiscuity

The pamphlet *Sexual health matters for young women* (HEA) explains that 'whether or not you have sex can be a difficult decision to make. But in the end it's what's right for you, and only you can answer that. If you've decided you're not ready for sex, then fine. Remember, it's your body, your choice and your right to say no. Only have sex because you want to'.[5] The young woman is offered a choice of whether or not to have sex, and her decision depends on what she *wants*, on her sexual desires, on how she feels at that moment in time, and not on any objective standard of right and wrong. Notice that if she does not *want* to have sex, then fine, it is her right to say no. The corollary is that if she does *want* to have sex then fine,

> Whether or not you have sex can be a difficult decision to make. But in the end it's what's right for you, and only you can answer that. If you've decided you're not ready for sex then fine.
>
> Remember, it's your body, your choice and your right to say no.
>
> **ONLY HAVE SEX BECAUSE YOU WANT TO**
>
> *Sexual health matters for young women* (HEA)

Remember, it's your body, your choice and your right to say no. Only have sex because you want to.

Lovelife (HEA)

it's her right to say yes. The inference is that whatever she chooses is right for her. So the message is that, when it comes to sexual behaviour, young people should do what they *want*. It is not difficult to see that this teaching leads to sexual anarchy, as each young person is encouraged to believe that they are free to do whatever they *want* to, whatever they feel to be right in their own eyes.

The pamphlet *Lovelife* (HEA) records the thoughts of a teenage virgin: 'Seventeen and the only virgin in my class – I thought I was the last person in the world who'd never had it. Everybody's doing it – maybe I should too.'[6] Here sex education is using the classic propaganda technique of the bandwagon effect. Everybody's doing 'it', so you should be doing 'it' too. Teenagers are actually being persuaded to follow the crowd and have sex. The pamphlet advises the young virgin that 'being prepared doesn't mean taking the fun out of sex. And it doesn't mean you are planning to sleep around. It just makes sense.' She is encouraged to buy condoms 'from a machine or in a supermarket where you can get them off the shelf with other goods. Once you've bought them a few times you'll find it much easier.' Teenagers are advised that 'if you're likely to be in a situation where you may have sex make sure you've got condoms with you.' This guidance gives a green light to promiscuous sex, for it suggests to impressionable teenagers that casual sex is fine provided they use a condom.

The booklet *Private & Confidential* (1994), published jointly by the British Medical Association, the Royal College of GPs, the FPA and Brook, has the aim of advising young girls under the age of 16 that they can get contraceptives from their GP without their parents knowing about it. Young girls are advised that 'it should be your choice to have sex. Think hard about the decision, don't jump into it before you're ready and never feel you have to do it because someone is pressuring you. It's really important to get contraception sorted out before you start having sex – or as early as possible in your relationship. Remember, you can get confidential help from a doctor even if you're under 16 so there's no need to take any risks.'[7] Notice the casual, amoral approach to promiscuous sex. Girls of 13, 14 and 15 are advised that they can choose to have sex if they *want* it. Notice the emphasis that under-age girls should make up their own mind about their sexual conduct, free no doubt from the influence of their parents or the teaching of the Church. One can only wonder how parents feel about this kind of advice being given to their daughters. Note too the false reassurance that 'there's no need to take any risks' – as if contraceptives remove all the risks associated with promiscuous sex.

'Seventeen and the only virgin in my class – I thought I was the last person in the world who'd never had it.'

'Everybody's doing it – maybe I should too.'

'I don't want to – but how do I say 'no'?'

Lovelife (HEA)

The guidance provided to our children by sex education is based on the morality of desire. The guiding principle is what a child *wants*. As there is no clear distinction between right and wrong in matters of sexual conduct, each child is free to develop his or her own moral framework. It is extraordinary that a country like the UK, which for centuries past has accepted the objective standard of biblical morality, should now teach children to develop their *own* set of values.

The 'safer sex' message

We have seen that teaching schoolchildren about contraception is at the heart of the Government's sex education strategy. Secondary schools are expected to give pupils full information about different types of contraception, including emergency contraception. Since 1994 it has been a legal requirement for state schools to provide information on 'safer sex' to help young people protect themselves against HIV and other sexually transmitted diseases.

The following examples illustrate the type of literature used to deliver

> "Some girls think that carrying condoms gives men the wrong idea. But lots of guys think it's a good thing – they want to share the responsibility of safer sex and they think it shows a sensible approach to sex."
>
> *Sexual health matters for young women* (HEA)

the Government's safer sex messages. The pamphlet, *Is Everybody Doing It? Your guide to contraception* (FPA), explains that an under-age child can get contraception from a doctor, family planning clinic or sexual health clinic. 'How old do I have to be? Any age. It doesn't matter how old you are or whether you are male or female. Many clinics run sessions for young people. Won't a doctor or nurse tell my parents I'm under 16? No. Even if you are under 16 doctors still have to keep anything you tell them private. Can a doctor or nurse refuse to give me contraception if I'm under 16? They can, but this is unlikely. The fact that you have asked for contraception shows that you have made a mature decision.' The pamphlet goes on: 'For safer sex use a condom. It can be embarrassing to suggest using condoms – particularly if you aren't sure how your partner feels about this or you haven't talked about it before. Perhaps you're worried they'll think it's a sign you've slept around – or that you think they've slept around!' The pamphlet then recites the 'safer sex' mantra: 'Condoms protect against both pregnancy and sexually transmitted infections. Condoms can keep both

Is Everybody Doing It? (FPA)

you and your partner safe and allow you to relax and enjoy sex.'[8] Notice that a child of *any* age can be provided with contraception without their parents' knowledge. In the eyes of the FPA the fact that an under-age child asks for contraception is regarded as a mature decision. The possibility that a girl of 12 or 13 is being groomed for promiscuous sex by a predatory man means nothing to the FPA.

According to the pamphlet *Lovelife* (HEA) 'only condoms

provide an "all-in-one" protection against pregnancy and sexually transmitted infections, including HIV'.[9] *Lovelife* continues, 'the best way to make sure that you don't have unprotected sex is to plan ahead' by making sure you've got condoms with you. 'It is better to be prepared than risk unsafe sex. After all, you can easily hide condoms in your pocket or purse.' And if you're in a situation where you may have sex, make sure you take your condoms. And if you're going abroad remember to buy your condoms before you go.[10] So all that a teenager has to do is get a free supply of condoms and she is prepared for her 'safer sex' adventures. But why the need to 'hide' her condoms? Is it because she feels guilty?

Say 'yes'? Say 'no'? Say 'maybe'? (Brook) provides teenagers with advice on using condoms. It explains that although everyone feels a bit silly using a condom for the first time, there are three ways to get around this. 'First, have a giggle – who says lovemaking has to be deadly serious? As long as you're not laughing at him but at the condom, nobody gets hurt. Buy one of the coloured condoms and make like it's a party. Second, get over your giggles by using condoms at other times and getting used to them. Blow them up at parties – see who can burst theirs first or who gets them biggest. Third, practice makes perfect. Girls can practise opening a packet and putting them on their partner (use a banana as a model), and boys can practise putting them on and wanking.'[11] And to encourage girls to take the initiative in buying condoms, they are informed that 'one condom in three is now bought by women, so girls needn't feel shy or odd buying them. Make it an initiative test – the first one of

"**What if my boyfriend won't buy them?**"

One condom in three is now bought by women, so girls needn't feel shy or odd buying them. Make it an initiative test - the first one of you to pluck up courage has to be given tickets for a gig !

"**I carry condoms - it 's the only smart thing to do**"

"**Think it over and do the right thing for you**"

"**My girlfriend thinks I'm the greatest - know why? 'Cos I use condoms and I'd never put her at risk!**"

Say yes? Say no? Say maybe?
(Brook)

Extracts from – *the cool lovers guide to condom use* (Brook)

you to pluck up courage has to be given tickets for a gig!'[12] Although the thought of teenage children playing party games with condoms is shocking to most parents, this is what children are being taught in the name of sex education.

The cartoon strip *the cool lovers guide to slick condom use* (Brook), aimed at 14 to 16 year-olds, shows Jon, a teenage boy, daydreaming about having sex with his girlfriend. When he realises that his girlfriend will expect him to practise 'safe sex', he searches for the condom attached to a leaflet he was given at the club. Jon mutters to himself, 'Now where's that "I'm a cool lover always carry a condom" gone?' Having found the mislaid condom the teenager comments, 'Let's have a practice run – I'd look a prat reading instructions in front of her'. The next day he tells his

Extracts from – *Play safe on holiday* (Brook)

girlfriend, 'I got some condoms. I wanted everything to be OK.' His girlfriend responds, 'I've got some too when I went to the clinic.' She tells Jon that she has also practised using them on a roll-on deodorant bottle, an experience she found 'ever so sexy'.[13] And so the two sexually aroused children are 'prepared' for sex. And it's all so easy, so sexy, so tragic.

The pamphlet *Play safe on holiday* (Brook), aimed at 14 to 16 year-olds, relates in cartoon strip the sexual adventures of two young women going on holiday. 'We'd saved all year for this holiday and nothing was going to stop us having a good time! Mandy had fallen straight into the arms of this guy (Jim) who'd sat next to us in the plane coming over.' After the second girl falls for Dan, one of the guys on the next balcony, the two young women get together to discuss their sexual adventures. 'I really fancy him, Mandy, but how on earth can I ask him to use a condom?' Mandy replies, with a happy smile, 'I've got all the colours of the rainbow with me – so I just asked Jim which he'd fancied!'[14] But her friend is despondent because Dan does not want to use a condom. 'It's no good – he thinks I think he's got something nasty! What shall I do?' Mandy advises her desperate friend, 'You could use a female condom yourself. Or you could play safe. Swimming naked together and massaging each other all over with suntan oil are about as sexy as you can get.' Notice the matter-of-fact way in which the pamphlet tells the reader that Mandy has already 'had sex' with Jim. The implication is that it is quite natural for a young girl to have casual sex with a man whom she has just met and, what's more, it is sensible for a young girl who is going on holiday to be armed with a range of condoms. And Mandy's happiness has come about because she was prepared for sex by carrying condoms. This pamphlet encourages lustful thoughts, promoting the idea of casual sex as the norm. Teenagers reading it are led to believe that it is quite acceptable, even expected, for young women on holiday to have a good time by indulging in sex with the first man who is willing, provided they 'play it safe' by using condoms.

Relationships and You, a Brook booklet produced with financial support from the Department of Health and Durex, advises teenagers how to make sex safer. According to the booklet, young people with access to clear and balanced facts should have 'the intelligence to carry a condom. Even if you have no intention of having sex for a good while yet, it's a smart move to be prepared. Condoms are the only form of contraception that protect against pregnancy and sexually transmitted infections. They can also be used along with other contraceptive methods, for extra protection.'[15] Notice the remarkable claim that, even for those who have no intention of having sex, to carry a condom is a sign of intelligence. Sex education, by linking condoms with the favourable word 'intelligence', is using a well known propaganda ploy. The inference is that a virgin who does not carry condoms is *not* intelligent. The reason she must 'be prepared', even if she has no intention of having sex, is because she has no control over her behaviour and so a sexual encounter may occur at any time.

Your Passport to Sexual Health, a booklet produced by Marie Stopes International, tells young people that 'a foreign holiday still holds promise of sun, sea and sex. But all too easily the romance can go sour, with irritating women's health problems and forgotten or lost contraceptives. Worse still, many women bring unwanted souvenirs home from their vacations – sexually transmitted diseases and unplanned pregnancies.'[16]

30

The booklet recommends that young people have their contraceptives sorted out two or three months before they go on holiday, and gives a few hints for a good time. 'The key to good holiday sexual health is condoms.' And 'condoms don't have to be a bore. They come in all colours, textures and flavours. They don't even have to smell rubbery – some condoms are made of plastic, making them thinner and stronger and odourless. Ask your GP or family planning clinic for free supplies of condoms. Then PACK THEM!!'[17] The advice continues, 'protection against pregnancy must be your first line of defence, but mistakes can happen. Condoms can come off or split, or you might just get carried away... But help is at hand. Emergency contraception can be used after unprotected sex.' And so Marie Stopes advises a young woman that to enjoy her holiday she needs to be well supplied with condoms, and even emergency contraception, in case her condoms fail.

The implicit message of these pamphlets is that casual sex is a lot of fun – it's quite usual to have sex after parties, after going to the pub or on holiday. The 'safer sex' message, however, seldom mentions the real danger of contraceptive failure. The sex educator does not emphasise the fact that condom failure rates of 14 per cent are reported in the medical literature.[18] In other words, with typical use 14 per cent of women will become pregnant over the course of a year. And failure rates among teenagers are likely to be even higher. This is why so many young girls who rely on 'safer sex' end up pregnant.

The ability of condoms to protect against STDs and HIV is even more doubtful. A workshop on the Scientific Evidence on Condom Effectiveness for STD Prevention, under the auspices of the National Institutes on Health in the USA, examined 138 research papers published in the scientific literature. An expert panel concluded: 'The ability to definitively demonstrate the presence or absence of a relationship between consistent and correct condom usage and the reduction in risk of STDs was significantly hampered by the lack of adequate study design in most, but not all studies under review.'[19] Because of the 'limitations in study designs there was insufficient evidence from the epidemiological studies on these diseases (gonorrhoea in women, chlamydial infection and trichomoniasis) to draw definite conclusions about the effectiveness of the latex male condom in

WHY WOULD I WANT TO USE A CONDOM?

You don't want to be a Dad just yet. Fatherhood is a big step!

WHY WOULD I WANT TO USE A CONDOM?

HOSPITAL

SEXUAL TRANSMITTED INFECTIONS CLINIC

You don't want to get (or pass on) any sexually transmitted infection like Chlamydia, genital warts, Herpes or HIV (the virus that causes AIDS). Especially as you can't usually tell if you or your partner has an infection.

You want to show your girlfriend/ partner that you can take your share of the responsibility for avoiding pregnancy or infection.

Roll with it! (Brook) The advice is misleading

reducing the transmission of these diseases'. It is estimated that 'consistent condom use decreased the risk of HIV/AIDS transmission by approximately 85%.'[20] This means that 15 out of 100 sexually active young people who rely on condoms for protection against HIV are at risk of acquiring the infection. Moreover, available epidemiological evidence 'does not allow an accurate assessment of the degree of protection against gonorrhoea infection in women offered by the correct and consistent condom use'.[21] There is no evidence that condoms provide protection against many other STDs, such as human papilloma virus, chlamydia or genital herpes.

In summary, the workshop on Condom Effectiveness, after studying the best available research, found no evidence that condoms prevent a number of sexually transmitted diseases. The 'safer sex' message that condoms provide all-in-one protection against STDs is a false claim. This is why there is now an epidemic in STDs among young people in the UK.

Homosexuality

The FPA believes that sex education 'should value all people equally, whether they be gay or lesbian, bisexual, heterosexual or transgendered. Understanding of and support for other people's sexual orientation should be actively promoted.'[22] The FPA's latest booklet, *Love, Sex, Relationships*, aimed at 13 to 16-year-olds, explains, 'Sexuality is a mix… What mix are you? A 'girly girl' who loves dressing in pink? A 'man's man' who loves lifting heavy weights? In practise, most of the world falls somewhere between these two extremes… You don't choose your sexual orientation – to be straight or gay, lesbian or bisexual – any more than you choose to be tall or small, black or white. It's just the way you are. Many parents and friends will support you, whatever your sexual orientation. If yours aren't supportive, there are plenty of people you can turn to who are (such as the London Lesbian and Gay Switchboard).'[23] The gender blender illustrates the notion of a sexual spectrum, with bisexuality the norm, and straight and gay at the extremes of the range. The idea that human sexuality is a continuous spectrum comes from the mindset of Alfred Kinsey,

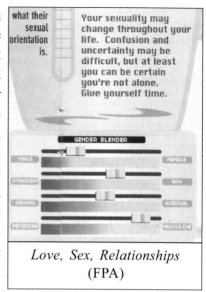

Love, Sex, Relationships
(FPA)

as we shall see on page 51. This theory is diametrically opposed to the biblical view that God created mankind male and female.

The booklet, *Is Everybody Doing It?* (FPA) gives this advice: 'Sexuality is not the same for everyone. Some people are attracted to people of the opposite sex, some to the same sex and some to both. Most people will grow up to be heterosexual (fancy someone of the opposite sex) but this doesn't mean that they are only attracted to the opposite sex all their lives.'[24] The FPA booklet *4Boys* gives teenagers the following advice. 'Getting an erection when you are around other boys doesn't mean that you are gay. But you may be sexually interested in other men – or even men AND women. It's not a problem; your body is yours to share with whomever you choose.'[25]

The pamphlet *Lovelife* informs young people that 'sexuality can be confusing at the best of times and if you're not sure which sex you're attracted to, you're not alone. Discovering your sexuality may take time, and you're the only one who can decide where your true feelings lie.' And if a teenager wants advice then they

I think I'm gay...
Getting an erection when you are around other boys doesn't mean that you are gay. But you may be sexually intersted in other men – or even men AND women. It's not a problem; your body is yours to share with whomever you choose.
If you want advice, contact the organisations on the back page.

4Boys (FPA)

I think I might be gay – who can I talk to?

Sexuality can be confusing at the best of times and if you're not sure which sex you're attracted to, you're not alone. Discovering your sexuality may take time, and you're the only one who can decide where your true feelings lie.

If you want a private chat with people who understand what you're going through, there are organisations such as the London Lesbian and Gay Switchboard who you can call on 020 7837 7324. They can give you information about local services.

Lovelife (HEA)

can phone the London Lesbian and Gay Switchboard for a private chat.[26]

Clearly sex education is promoting a homosexual agenda among children, propagating the idea that both homosexuality and bisexuality are natural and should not be regarded as a problem. It is up to young people to choose with whom they want to share their body. And if they want to be sexually active with members of both sexes, then that is their choice, and nobody has the right to judge them. Sex education makes no moral distinction between heterosexual and homosexual sex – both are equally acceptable, it's simply a matter of choice.

Sex education, marriage and the family

Sex education ideology is profoundly anti-marriage. The FPA policy statement on sex education does not mention marriage, and neither does most sex education literature. In other words, children are taught about sex in a framework that does not recognise marriage as important. Consequently, children are led to believe that sex outside marriage is the acceptable norm. This point is illustrated in an article written by a teacher, Susan Elkin, who is brave enough to report what is actually happening in some schools. She explains how the head of science asked her to teach a sex education module to a class of 14 and 15-year-olds. She was provided with a pile of worksheets and a box of contraceptive samples, and given the task of teaching the children the mechanics of contraception, with the clear instruction, 'We don't, as a matter of policy, mention marriage or use the terms "husband" or "wife".'[27]

The FPA believes that sex education 'should recognise and appreciate the value and diversity of families that exist and should not value one family structure as superior to another'.[28] To help primary school teachers with their sex education lessons, *Healthwise*, a Liverpool based voluntary organisation, has produced *The Primary School Sex and Relationships Education Pack*. The introduction explains that, 'In the past some people have suggested narrow, moralistic aims for sex education. This has included suggestions such as promoting marriage in the family, dissuading children from having sex before marriage, telling children what is right and wrong etc., in a manner which has more to do with propaganda than with education.'[29] Under the heading 'families and parenting', the resource pack explains that teachers should tell children aged 7 to 11 that families come in many different forms. Children are shown a picture of six different types of 'family' – two children with their mother and father, two children with mother and stepfather, one child with her single mother, one child with her grandparents, one child living with a foster family, and two children living with their mum and her lesbian partner. Children are invited to choose one of the families and to write a story about it. The class is then asked to discuss the advantages and disadvantages of being married in a non-judgemental way. The message that is being imparted to children is that there are many types of family and the traditional family of father, mother and children is simply one arrangement, no better or worse than any other 'family' arrangement.

The idea that sex education is trying to get across to schoolchildren is that there are many different forms of family, *all of which have equal moral validity*, including a same-sex family, stepfamily and single parent family. According to Sarah Gammage, in an essay on *The Teaching of Sexuality*, 'Teachers cannot, and should not, teach children that the only acceptable form of family is that of mother, father and children. This would be to deny that the experience of love, care and responsibility are possible without this configuration of people. It would be gross insensitivity toward the backgrounds of pupils.'[30]

The above analysis leaves no doubt that the message of sex education is profoundly hostile to the traditional family. In *The triumph of the thera-peutic: uses of faith after Freud*, Philip Reiff came to the conclusion: 'Sex education becomes the main weapon in an ideological war against the family; its aim was to divest the parents of their moral authority. Sex education is meant to replace the moral authority of the family with that of the state, acting through its primary agent, the public school system.'[31] What is deeply disturbing is that the British Government is content to use the national curriculum as an ideological weapon to indoctrinate children against the biblical teaching of marriage and the traditional family, a teaching that has been accepted by the vast majority of the population for centuries.

Endnotes

1 Hansard. Lords debate, 9 March 1994, cc1423-1426

2 *Daily Telegraph*, 26 March 1994, letter, Smut posing as sex education, Valerie Riches

3 *Daily Telegraph*, 25 March 1994, Smutty guide casts cloud over future of sex education authority, Philip Johnson and Peter Pallot

4 *Daily Telegraph*, 30 March 1994, Sex advisers back booklet minister banned, Peter Pallot

5 *Sexual matters for young women*, Health Education Authority, inside front cover

6 *Lovelife* - sexual health for young people, Health Education Authority, p2

7 *Private & Confidential - talking to doctors*, The British Medical Association, General Medical Services Committee, Royal College of General Practitioners, Brook Advisory Centres and the Family Planning Association, 1994

8 *Is Everybody Doing It? Your guide to contraception*, Family Planning Association, 2000, p7

9 Ibid. *Lovelife*, p4

10 Ibid. p6, p8

11 *Say 'yes'? Say 'no'? Say 'maybe'?*, Suzie Hayman, Brook 1999, p13

12 Ibid. p16

13 *The cool lovers guide to slick condom use*, leaflet, Brook publications

14 *Play safe on holiday*, leaflet, Brook publications

15 *Relationships and You*, Making Sex Safer, Brook, p36

16 *Your Passport to Sexual Health*, Marie Stopes International, p1

17 Ibid. p6

18 *Contraceptive Efficiency*, J Trussell in *Contraceptive Technology*, BMJ Books, 1998, p800

19 Workshop on Scientific Evidence on Condom Effectiveness for STD Prevention, June 12-13th 2000, USA Agency for International Development, Food and Drug Administration, Centers for Disease Control and Prevention, National Institute of Health, p27

20 Ibid. p14

21 Ibid. p16

22 FPA policy statement, Sex and relationship education (SRE), January 2006, fpa website

23 *Love, Sex, Relationships*, Family Planning Association, 2005, pp 6–7

24 *Is Everybody Doing It?* Family Planning Association, 2000, p2

25 *4Boys*, Family Planning Association, 2000, p13

26 Ibid. *Lovelife*, p27

27 *Daily Telegraph*, 12 January 1994, Education: In my view – the moral side of sex, Susan Elkin

28 Ibid. FPA policy statement on SRE

29 The Primary School Sex & Relationships Education Pack, Healthwise publications, 1999 edition

30 Sarah Gammage, *The Teaching of Sexuality*, in Children and controversial issues, ed Bruce Carrington and Barry Troyna, The Falmer Press, p200

31 Philip Reiff, *The triumph of the therapeutic: uses of faith after Freud*, Harper & Row, 1966, cited from 'The Sex Education Fraud' by Chuch Morse, website chuchmorse.com

4

Talking about sex

A key aim of sex education is to help children and young people talk about sex. According to the Government's guidance, 'It is essential that schools can help children and young people develop confidence in talking, listening and thinking about sex and relationships. Teachers and other staff may need to overcome their own anxieties and embarrassment to do this effectively.'[1] The inference is that it is important for teachers and children to overcome their natural sense of embarrassment so that they feel comfortable talking openly about sex. In addition, parents are being persuaded that they should learn to discuss sex with their children in an open and frank way, always stressing the importance of 'safe sex'.

Talking about condoms

Young people are advised to 'talk about condoms before it's too late'. According to *Sexual health matters for young women* (HEA) it can be difficult to raise the subject of condoms. 'Mention condoms too early and you might feel you look pushy or available. But the earlier you discuss it, the less likely you are to get carried away and end up not using any protection. If you discuss protection with your partner early on it will be easier to agree on safer sex, or to change your mind about having sex at all if you don't feel happy. You could talk about episodes in soaps, TV programmes or magazine articles involving sex and steer the conversation around to safer sex. You can then let your partner know what you think and see how they feel too. If you both decide you want to have sex, make sure you have safer sex. So use a condom. If you can't find the right words to talk about it, you could try one of these ideas. Wait until you're both undressing and then casually ask "Your condoms or mine?" It's easier to

Condom talk

A lot of women are scared to say:
"Use a condom."

You've bought the condoms but how do you suggest using one? It can be difficult to raise the subject. Mention condoms too early and you might feel you look pushy or available. But the earlier you discuss it, the less likely you are to get carried away and end up not using any protection.

If you discuss protection with your partner early on it will be easier to agree on safer sex, or to change your mind about having sex at all if you don't feel happy.

You could talk about episodes in soaps, TV programmes or magazine articles involving sex and steer the conversation around to safer sex. You can then let your partner know what you think and see how they feel too.

Sexual health matters for young women (HEA)

do this when you've still got your underwear on and you're not in any danger of getting carried away'[2]

The pamphlet *Lovelife* explains, 'You've bought the condoms – now how do you suggest using one? Talking about safer sex doesn't have to be difficult. Once you mention it you might find your partner is just as keen to talk about it as you are.'[3]

But why is it so difficult to talk about condoms and 'safer sex'? Because young people have a natural sense of embarrassment that tells them that they are entering into forbidden territory. They know in their conscience that thinking and talking openly about condoms and promiscuous sex is wrong and they feel ashamed. Sex education, however, seeks to overcome their natural sense of shame. It wants a society of shameless, sexually liberated young people who no longer know how to blush, for then they will gladly receive the messages of 'safer sex'. Once young people lose their sense of shame they are in danger of falling into a lifestyle given over to sexual immorality.

Parents talking about sex

The FPA booklet *Talking to your child about sex* (1998) explains that 'children need to learn about the positive side of sex as well as being aware of risks and dangers. Showing children that it's alright to talk about sex gives them a positive message.' And to overcome embarrassment parents are told to 'introduce the topic when your child is very young… if you show your child that you are happy to talk about sex, relationships and feelings, they will know they can ask questions about anything they don't understand.'[4] If we don't talk to our children about sex they pick up the message that sex is scary and shouldn't be talked about.[5] The booklet admits that it's embarrassing to talk to children about sex. All parents know that. 'It's OK to go red and tell your child you're embarrassed. You can help your child learn about sex even if you don't feel very comfortable talking about it.' And the earlier you start the better.

The FPA booklet points out that the real problem arises with older children because teenagers often find it much harder to talk to their parents about sex. 'If your children say they know all about sex, just ask them what they know – and fill in the gaps.' And then we get to the difficult bit, explaining sexual responsibility to our children. 'You will need to explain that being responsible about sexual behaviour means considering the needs and feelings of the partner, and discussing the kind of relationship both partners want.

> If you both decide you want to have sex, make sure you have safer sex. So use a condom. If you can't find the right words to talk about it, you could try one of these ideas.
>
> * Wait until you're both undressing and then casually ask "Your condoms or mine?" It's easier to do this when you've still got your underwear on and you're not in any danger of getting emotionally and physically carried away.
>
> * Say "We need to use a condom. I would never make love without one."
>
> * Say "I'd like to use a condom: better safe than sorry."
>
> For more information about condoms, read the HEA's leaflet *The condom guide: making sex safer* (see p.19).
>
> For more information on sexual health matters for young women and men, turn this booklet upside down and see page 6.
>
> **TALK CONDOMS BEFORE IT'S TOO LATE**
>
> *Sexual health matters for young women* (HEA)

It means not having sex if one's partner isn't ready. If both partners decide to make love, it means being able to talk about safer sex to avoid sexually transmitted infections, and using contraception unless they both want a baby.'[6]

The booklet, however, does not advise parents to talk to their children about marriage, neither does it advise them to explain the dangers of sexual promiscuity; it does not even mention the great value of teaching children the discipline of self-control. Instead, parents are encouraged to teach their children that sexual responsibility means using contraception, and parents are expected to be supportive if their son or daughter and their partner 'decide to make love'.

The Government's *Teenage Pregnancy* report claims that parents' reluctance to talk to their children about sex is a major reason for the high incidence of teenage sexual tragedies, and to overcome this deficiency

SRE & Parents

Some useful values statements to think about when talking with your child:

- Have sex with someone you really care about and who will share responsibility for contraception and safer sex.

- It would be better to wait to have sex until you are old enough to take responsibility.

- Families have different beliefs about sex, sometimes these are guided by the religion that they follow.

- Sex should never be used to exploit someone.

SRE & Parents (Department for Education and Skills)

the Department of Health has commissioned a national campaign to help parents talk to their children about sex.[7]

The leaflet *SRE & Parents* (2001), produced by the Department for Education and Skills, has been written to persuade parents to take a more active role in the sex education of their children. The leaflet suggests 'some useful values statements' for parents to think about when talking with their children. For example, a mother may say to her daughter, 'Have sex with someone you really care about and who will share responsibility for contraception and safer sex.' Or a mother may say, 'It would be better to wait to have sex until you are old enough to take responsibility.'[8] The inference is that parents should persuade their children that responsible behaviour means using contraception. In other words, parents should encourage their children to practise 'safer sex'. There is no advice that parents should teach their children that sexual activity should be reserved for marriage.

The campaign to encourage parents to talk to their children about sex is contrary to biblical teaching. The Bible instructs parents to bring their children up in the training and instruction of the Lord, teaching them the moral standards by which they ought to live, emphasising sexual purity and modesty. There must be no unwholesome talk (Ephesians 4:29) and the use of filthy language is strictly forbidden (Colossians 3:8). Exposing children to sex talk is unnatural, an assault on the innocence of childhood and a subtle form of child abuse. Moreover, because of the moral imperative that surrounds sexual behaviour, children can only be confused and embarrassed by the crass attempts of their parents to talk about sex. Most children are deeply embarrassed by the thought of discussing sex and condoms with their mother or father.

Sex words

According to the sex educators even young children need a sexual vocabulary, and the larger the vocabulary the more they will feel able to talk about sex. An FPA training manual, *The weird and wonderful world of Billy Ballgreedy*, acknowledges that 'talking about issues relating to sex is often unfamiliar and uncomfortable for young people, invariably causing much embarrassment and laughter'. But the FPA has a technique for overcoming this embarrassment – the sex words brainstorm. The sex educator allocates children into a number of small groups with a sheet of flip chart paper divided into four sections. They are asked to write a 'sex' word in each section, and then to think of as many alternative 'sex' words as possible. Nothing is off limits, for sex education does not recognise the concept of foul language. The groups are asked to call out all their words, and the group with the highest number is declared the winner.[9] Another game provides children with a jumbled set of display cards with half a sex word on each. They are set the task of matching the cards to complete the sex words. The aim of these games is to empower children to use sex language without any sense of embarrassment. Nothing is taboo, and nothing is too embarrassing. The purpose is to desensitise children against sexual embarrassment; to overcome their sense of shame and extinguish their natural inhibitions. Eventually, when they are fully desensitised, they will be able to talk freely and openly about sex.

Sexual images

Another dimension of sex education is to teach children in a way that is blatant and explicit. Many sex education films, books and pamphlets provide children with graphic visual images of the sexual organs, and it is now

ON HOW TO USE A CONDOM

Is Everybody Doing It? (FPA)

widely accepted that displaying the sexual organs is simply part of a child's education. Most are so explicit it would be indecent to show examples in this book. Brook's booklet *A look at safe sex*, contains detailed, explicit, close-up, drawings of the sexual organs, including an explicit, realistic drawing of a condom being fitted to an erect penis. The inside cover of the FPA booklets *4Boys* and *4Girls* use realistic drawings to show frontal views of a row of naked young men and women. *Is Everybody Doing It?* provides hot tips on how to use a condom in careful graphic detail. The caption 'put on a condom as soon as the penis is fully erect and before it touches the vagina' is illustrated with a realistic drawing of an erect penis.[10] A series of drawings show how to roll a condom all the way down to the base of the penis, how to keep the condom in place while withdrawing – 'do this slowly and carefully so no semen is spilt' – and how the condom should be wrapped and put in a bin. Many of the explicit images used by sex education would be labelled pornographic by most parents.

Sex education literature is full of suggestive sexual innuendoes. The cover of *Love, Sex, Relationships* (FPA) shows a group of young people on a roller coaster ride. In the front coaster is a man with both hands on the breasts of the woman sitting next to him. The suggestion is that it is

Love, Sex, Relationships (FPA)

quite acceptable for young men to touch the breasts of young women. *4Girls* shows a young man lying on a sofa fondling the breasts of his girlfriend.

The condom demonstrator is an essential tool of the sex educator. Children are taught to unroll condoms on a realistic model of an erect penis. And all this must be done with no sense of shame, for children are only truly liberated when all things sexual are in the open. Sex must be uncovered and exposed; nothing is to be

GOING FURTHER

My boyfriend says I'm frigid because I don't want to have sex. **Frigid** is an insulting word used when girls say 'no'. If he's interested in you he'd be prepared to listen to how you feel and wait if necessary. If he isn't, he's just putting pressure on you. Sex should be enjoyable, so:

● **Don't** have sex until you're absolutely sure it's what you want.
● **Ditch** boys who try to pressure you or insult you.
● **Realise** that all women can enjoy sex with the right partner at the right time.

4Girls (FPA)

hidden, nothing is private, nothing is sacred – all is exposed in the name of sex education. Shameless sex educators aim to create shameless children who have images of the sexual organs imprinted in their impressionable minds.

In the last 40 years, since the advent of sex education, there has been a radical change in what society accepts as sexual decency. We have moved from a society that believed in modesty to a society that glorifies sexual explicitness. Lord Longford was right – sex education has succeeded in legitimising pornography.

Embarrassment

The promotion of sexually explicit words and images among mixed groups of children undermines modesty in girls and chivalry in boys. Teaching girls to use sex words, to view sexual images, and to unroll condoms onto a dildo, is to demean their modesty and dishonours them in front of other children. The assumption that girls need to know about contraception creates the impression in the fertile imagination of the boys that they cannot wait to become sexually active. The girls are placed in a situation where they appear to be interested in sex, and in the minds of the boys they become sex objects. What do boys think of the girl who follows the advice of sex education to carry condoms, even though she claims to have no intention of having sex for a good while yet? What excuse can any girl have for not agreeing to have sex with her boyfriend when she is supposed to know all about 'safe sex'? And what girl who has practised unrolling condoms can pretend to be modest? These girls are trapped – they are being groomed for a life of promiscuous sex. This is state-sponsored child abuse.

Boys are being introduced to ideas and images that expose them to unnatural sexual thoughts and inflame sexual lust. Any thought of chivalry and respect towards girls has been blown away. Suddenly the idea that they can have sex with a schoolgirl becomes a distinct possibility. In the minds of the boys the girls have become potential sex objects, for they know about sex and how to prevent pregnancy. The gateway to promiscuity is opened wide. It is not difficult to see that sexual explicitness arouses lust and leads to sexual temptation. When modesty is destroyed, girls lose their innocence and become sexually available, the objects of pleasure, to be used and discarded. Casual sex becomes the norm for there are no restraints. Sex is no longer an intensely private matter between husband and wife, but a trivialised game, a plaything, something to give pleasure to lustful males. When young men lose respect for women they become predators who feel entitled to satisfy their sexual lusts.

Parental responsibility

It is the responsibility of all parents, Christian and non-Christian alike, to teach their children a moral framework on which to base their lives, and this is especially true when it comes to sexual conduct. God's laws are righteous and good. The Bible commands parents to take every opportunity to teach God's moral law to their children. Even among those who are not practising Christians, many still want their children to be taught the basics of biblical morality.

Parents should teach their children our Lord's standard of sexual purity, the meaning and purpose of marriage and the biblical virtues of modesty, chivalry, self-control, chastity and fidelity. (The leaflet, *The divine plan for sexual conduct*, included as an appendix, provides a good framework for teaching the biblical view of sexual conduct.) The first nine chapters of Proverbs can be used to teach children that true wisdom is found in God's word. Young people are to be warned to flee the evil desires of youth (2 Timothy 2:22). The perils of sexual immorality must be explained, for playing with sex is playing with fire. Can a young man scoop fire into his lap without burning his clothes? Can a man walk on hot coals and not burn his feet? (Proverbs 6). The book of Titus is used to teach children the great value of self-control and the importance of saying no to ungodliness and worldly passions (Titus 2). Parents should show their children that the Bible condemns sexual impurity, fornication, adultery, incest, homosexuality, filthy language and coarse joking.

Those children who understand the value of chastity and self-control will want no part of sex education. They will object to being told about contraceptive techniques and how to 'be prepared' for sex. Those children who understand our Lord's standard of sexual purity will condemn the explicit sexual images of sex education as pornographic, and will object to being taught a vocabulary of sex words.

Endnotes

1 *Sex and relationship education guidance*, DfEE, July 2000, p22
2 *Sexual health matters for young women*, Heath Education Authority, p5
3 *Lovelife*, Heath Education Authority, p7
4 *Talking to your child about sex*, Family Planning Association, 7/98
5 Ibid.
6 Ibid.
7 *Teenage Pregnancy*, HMSO, London, June 1999, p95
8 *SRE & Parents*, DfES publications, 0706/2001
9 *The weird and wonderful world of Billy Ballgreedy support manual*, Family Planning Association, Matthew Crozier
10 *Is Everybody Doing It?* Family Planning Association, 2000, p8

5

The sexual revolution

How ironic that after three decades of free contraception for children, provided free by the state, and after a massive Government inspired sex education campaign promoted by millions of leaflets and pamphlets, the UK has the highest rate of teenage pregnancies in Western Europe! How ironic that after three decades of free condoms for children and a massive 'safer sex' campaign there is now an epidemic of sexually transmitted diseases among young people! Any reasonable person would conclude that the policy has failed, that the promotion of contraceptives is not the answer to teenage sexual tragedies. Why then does our Government persist with the policy of promoting contraceptives among children, a policy that is clearly not meeting its stated objectives?

To answer this question we need to understand the real objective of sex education. To do so we need to explore the link between sex education and the sexual revolution. In my book *Lessons in Depravity* I conclude, 'we can only understand the motivation behind sex education if we grasp the essential point that sex education has evolved out of the ideas of the sexual revolution'.[1] Many of the revolutionaries, whose aim was to liberate society from the repressive moral standards of the Christian faith, realised that sex education could be a powerful vehicle for promoting their ideas among children.

Friedrich Nietzsche

In the last two decades of the 19th century the German philosopher Friedrich Nietzsche developed a new way of thinking that was a direct assault on Christian morality. His boast was that, as one of the early revolutionaries, he was the original immoralist. He saw the Christian faith as the enemy of mankind and totally rejected biblical morality. The *Encyclopaedia*

Britannica assesses Nietzsche's criticism of Christianity as follows: 'At bottom the charge is always the same: Christianity is born of weakness, failure and resentment and is the enemy of reason and honesty, of the body and of sex in particular, and of power, joy and freedom.'[2]

His proclamation that God was dead led to the notion that there is no objective truth, and therefore no absolute moral standard. Having removed the absolute moral laws of the Bible, people are free to decide their own values, to set their own standards. Because there is no objective moral truth, it follows that what I *want*, if it makes me feel good, is right for me at that moment. His thinking introduced the ideas that would develop into the ideology of post-modernism, in which each person is free to decide their own truth and their own morality.

This philosophy opened the gateway for the sexual revolution. As we have seen, sex education advice is based on Nietzsche's amoral philosophy – 'Remember, it's your body, your choice and your right to say no. Only have sex because you *want* to. But in the end it's what's right for you, and only you can answer that. If you and your partner decide you both *want* to have sex, then fine. There's a lot of new things to think about such as contraception.' Sex education, following Nietzsche's atheistic world-view, encourages the idea that young people, and even children, are free to develop their own set of sexual values, without regard to God's moral law.

Sigmund Freud

Sigmund Freud took up the baton of promoting an amoral world-view from Nietzsche. His voluminous writings have had a massive influence on Western thought. At the heart of Freud's work was his hostility to the Christian faith, and his motivation was to provide an interpretation of human sexuality that disregarded biblical morality.

In all his writings there is not the slightest suggestion that any sexual act is wrong or immoral, for his theories had succeeded in demoralising sexual behaviour. People are driven by unconscious sexual desires over which they have little control, and suppressing these desires is supposed to cause neurosis. Freud explained life in terms of the sexual impulse, the libido, which is bisexual in direction. His greatest discovery was uncovering infantile sexuality. In his mind, children from the earliest ages have hidden desires to have sex with their parents, an idea that was to be developed and expounded by Alfred Kinsey.

Freud's theory has contributed substantially to the corruption of sexual morals in the modern world. It is now orthodoxy to think that children are sexual beings. According to academic philosopher Roger Scruton: 'These assumptions underlie the repulsive lessons in sex education that the national curriculum is now forcing on children – lessons designed to facilitate sexual activity long before personal love is possible...'[3]

Freud's contribution to human thought was to separate sex from human love, marriage and reproduction. After he had pronounced his theories, people were encouraged to think about sex as an instinctive force, and to do so without any moral constraints – the gateway to the sexual revolution was opened even wider.

Marie Stopes

It is probably true to say that the sex education movement in England started with the publication of Marie Stopes' book *Married Love* in 1918. Her contribution to the sexual revolution was to cultivate the myth of sexual ignorance and to legitimise the use of sexually explicit language. She propagated the idea that the public was ignorant about sex and this ignorance could only be overcome by explicit sexual information. As an expert propagandist she used every means of publicity to promote her ideas. The effect of her writings was to undermine modesty in the minds of those who read her books. Her other contribution to the revolution was to found the Family Planning Association, the organisation that is now in the forefront of the sex education movement.

The organisation that bears her name, Marie Stopes International, is now active in 35 countries promoting the ideals of the sexual revolution. It has moved a long way from her original claim that she was promoting contraception for the benefit of married couples. The organisation's website, in response to the question 'is there a right time to have sex for the first time', advises young people to 'have sex when you really feel ready, never mind what anyone else says'. A slogan of Marie Stopes International is 'Cover the world with condoms'.

Wilhelm Reich

The author of *The Sexual Revolution*, Wilhelm Reich, a disciple of Freud, claimed that Christian teaching on sexual conduct was the cause of sexual oppression. As a dedicated advocate of sexual liberation he outlined the objectives of the revolution in stark terms. He asserted that at the heart of a sexually repressed society is the institution of marriage and what he referred to as the authoritarian family. Marriage was a major obstacle in the way of the revolution, for it acted as the brake on sexual liberation, helping to maintain chastity and marital fidelity. The family is the main vehicle for giving children a traditional moral foundation and this helps to perpetuate sexual repression. So for the revolution to succeed marriage and the traditional family must be destroyed, for only then can there be true sexual liberation.

Perhaps Reich's greatest contribution to the revolution was to recognise the potential of explicit sex education for inculcating into the minds of children the ideals of sexual freedom. He understood the power of nakedness as a weapon in the battle against Christian morality. He realised that children exposed to explicit sexual images would have difficulty in accepting biblical teaching on sexual purity and modesty. He saw that sex education could be used as a pretext for introducing children to explicit images that would be unthinkable in any other arena. Reich's dogma that explicit images are an essential part of sex education has gained full acceptance in the UK.

Alfred Kinsey

The publication of Kinsey's reports on human sexual behaviour in the early 1950s heralded a major advance for the sex revolutionaries. *Esquire* magazine referred to Alfred Kinsey as the patron saint of sex, the man whose reports set in motion the first wave of the sexual revolution. There is no doubt that Kinsey's research has had a massive impact on public morality and the popular understanding of human sexual behaviour. It has also had a powerful and far-reaching influence on sex education policy in the USA and the UK.

In *Kinsey, Sex and Fraud* (1990) Judith Reisman and her co-authors document the sinister spirit behind the work of Kinsey. 'In view of Kinsey's

Play safe

If you both decide you do want to have sex, the chances are you'll both want to reduce the risk of unwanted pregnancy and protect each other from sexual infections.

If you or your partner use a reliable method of contraception the risk of unintended pregnancy is low, but you both share the responsibility.

Sexual infections are very common. Used properly, condoms can help protect against them. If you have sex without a condom with someone who is already infected, you risk getting a sexual infection including HIV, the virus which causes AIDS (see p.13).

The chances are neither you nor your partner may know if you have a sexual infection. That's why it's better to practise safer sex than take a risk. It's not about lack of trust – it's just playing safe.

PLAY IT SAFE

Sexual health matters for young men (HEA)

grossly and knowingly unrepresentative interviewee populations, his use of data from illegal sexual experimentation on children, his history of deception in other endeavours, his predetermined bias and selection of like-minded co-researchers, his unethical and deceptive omission of data injurious to his own hypotheses, and his lucky coincidence in finding out about human sexuality exactly what he wanted to find out, we believe Kinsey's research to be worse than worthless – we believe the evidence overwhelmingly points to fraud.'[4]

Kinsey was not an objective scientist, as he claimed, but a dedicated sexual revolutionary. At the centre of his research was a fascination with the sexual response of children. He cultivated the idea that even the youngest children are sexually responsive and therefore sexual contacts with adults are a source of pleasure to some children. He argued that if adolescent children are not sexually active, this is because of 'parental or social repressions of the growing child'.[5] Kinsey's research provided the 'scientific' foundation for the belief that children benefit from becoming sexually active at an early age – with the help of adult 'partners'.[6]

At the heart of Kinsey's ideology is a profound rejection of biblical morality. Sex is no more than a natural biological instinct and therefore sexual choices should be free from moral inhibitions. His approach is strictly amoral; nothing is right or wrong, no form of sexual outlet is abnormal or harmful and there is no such thing as sexual perversion for every type of sexual activity, even homosexuality and bestiality, are natural. He envisaged a world free from traditional moral restraints that have in the past prevented people from expressing their 'true' sexual nature.

Kinsey developed a heterosexual-homosexual rating scale, which showed human sexuality as a continuum, with bisexuality as the norm. He had manipulated 'scientific' evidence to 'prove' that human beings are actually bisexual by nature. His perverted theory of human sexuality lies at the heart of sex education policy in the UK (see gender-blender pages 32 and 33).

Characteristics of the sexual revolution

We can now summarise the essential characteristics of the sexual revolution, for this will help us see how it relates to sex education.
1. The sexual revolution is a rebellion against the moral law of God. The revolutionaries have rejected the God of the Bible and His moral law.
2. Because there is no moral law, no form or type of sexual activity is wrong or depraved and there is no such thing as sexual immorality. It follows that people are free to do what they believe to be right in their own eyes, and to set their own standards of sexual behaviour.
3. Human sexuality is a continuum with bisexuality the norm. It follows that same-sex relationships are perfectly natural. Biblical truth that God created mankind as two distinct sexes, male and female in the image of God, is ignored.
4. The traditional family is a cause of sexual repression. Biblical teaching that sexual activity should take place only in marriage between a man and his wife is rejected. Casual sex is the norm.
5. Christian virtues of modesty and self-control inhibit sexual enjoyment. Sexual explicitness helps people achieve true sexual liberation.

The real objective of sex education

There is no doubt that the sex education industry has been spectacularly unsuccessful in achieving its stated aims, and not even the most ideologically blind can still believe that contraceptive-based sex education is the answer. So the mantra – condoms reduce teenage pregnancies, abortions and sexually transmitted infections – appears to have been a smokescreen to obscure the real objectives of sex education.

So what are the *real* objectives of sex education? *The truth is that sex education is little more than the propaganda arm of the sexual revolution.* The real objective of sex education is, and always has been, to destroy traditional morality and promote the amoral ideology of the sexual revolution. In this, it has been remarkably successful. The characteristics of sex education, therefore, are similar to those of the sexual revolution, and can be summed up in the following points:

1. The real objective of sex education is to demoralise sexual conduct in the eyes of children. Sex education is amoral—no type of sexual behaviour is wrong or immoral, and moralising is a serious error.

2. When it comes to sexual behaviour, children must decide for themselves whether or not to have sex, and whatever choice they make is right for them. If they want to have sex, then fine, provided they use a condom.

3. Explicit images and language make children more open to the messages of 'safer sex' by undermining their natural sense of embarrassment. Explicitness aims to destroy the virtue of modesty.

4. There is nothing special about marriage, for all types of sexual relationship are equally valid. Sex outside marriage, even among children, is the norm.

5. Sex education is hostile to the traditional family created by marriage.

6. Children are helped to find their true sexual orientation. Some are sexually attracted to both males and females, but this is not a problem for bisexuality is the norm and same-sex relationships are natural.

It is not difficult to see that sex education is a weapon in the hands of those who are promoting a revolution against God's standard of sexual behaviour. Our children and grandchildren are being indoctrinated into the amoral ideology of the sexual revolution. They are the targets of a massive state-sponsored propaganda campaign against biblical morality. May God help them.

Endnotes

1 ES Williams, *Lessons in Depravity*, Belmont House Publishing, London, 2003, p241

2 *Encyclopaedia Britannica*, Nietzsche, Friedrich, William Benton, 1963, vol. 16, p435

3 *Sunday Times*, 8 April 2001, News Review, Dr Fraud, Roger Scruton

4 Judith Reisman, Edward Eichel, John Court, Gordon Muir, *Kinsey, Sex and Fraud*, A Lochinvar-Huntington House Publication, 1990, p219

5 Alfred Kinsey, Wardell Pomeroy, Clyde Martin, *Sexual Behavior in the Human Male*, WB Saunders Company, 11th printing 1953, p180

6 Ibid. Judith Reisman, *Kinsey, Sex and Fraud*, p217

6

The great Christian compromise

As we survey the scene of sexual devastation that is being visited on the children of our nation, what is the Christian response? Who cares that biblical morality is being traduced in the eyes of our children? In my view, the Christian witness has been ineffective because of a widespread reluctance to use biblical truth to oppose the amoral ideology that drives sex education.

It is unwise for Christians to discuss sexual conduct without reference to God's word, for it alone has the authority to distinguish right from wrong. As sex education deals with moral issues, it must be approached from within the moral framework of biblical revelation. Because God's moral law is good and righteous it has a powerful appeal to the human heart. In our postmodern society there is a growing hunger for truth, for many people know that the Bible provides the standard by which we ought to live. Most parents want their children to be taught the difference between right and wrong and are delighted when the Church gives a clear moral lead and pronounces unequivocally that promiscuity and homosexuality are wrong.

Unfortunately there are few Christians who are prepared to tackle the moral evils associated with sex education. On the contrary, most Christians accept, without any biblical justification, the view that children need sex education and so the challenge is to find a sensitive 'Christian' version. My research has shown that many evangelical Christian organisations are teaching sexual matters in a way that is little different from secular sex educators. They have fallen into the trap of demoralising sexual conduct. Consequently, the so-called 'Christian' versions of sex education are inconsistent with biblical morality. Some of the materials used in the name of the Christian faith are dishonouring to the gospel of truth.

CARE's sex education

The leading Christian organisation involved in sex education is CARE (Christian Action, Research and Education). It claims that although there is a debate in society as to the best methods of reducing teenage pregnancies, 'there is no doubt that schools are recognised as having a part to play. Sex education is not an issue that can be ignored!'[1] CARE's booklet *Your School and Sex Education* (1996) has been written 'to help teachers, parents and governors who are involved in discussions about sex education or are concerned with the task of producing, revising or reviewing a school sex education policy'.[2] The document makes it clear that its intention is not to discuss the pros and cons of the Government's guidance, only to clarify what schools are required to do. It has since been revised and published as *Sex and Relationship Education* (2001).[3]

In my research for *Lessons in Depravity*, a book which documents the link between sex education and the sexual revolution, I viewed CARE's video *Make Love Last*. I could not believe what I was seeing. Here was a video produced by a Christian organisation, and widely used by secondary schools, that contained smutty foul language. The central character, Randy Factor, asks a group of young people whether they are 'putting it around a bit, you know, dipping your wick'. Randy uses phrases like, 'You need to get bonking fit'; 'pumping for humping'; 'leg-over time'; 'the more I score the better I score' and 'the sponsored bonk'. And worse, children are offered advice on sexual conduct by the agony aunt of the salacious magazine *Just 17*. (See page 22, *Your Pocket Guide to Sex*). The whole ethos is to trivialise sexual conduct. And this is supposed to be a Christian response to amoral secular sex education! Clearly there is something profoundly wrong with CARE's approach to sex education.

CARE's training manual *Parents First – Sex education within the home* is so important that church leaders are encouraged to incorporate it into their teaching programme. CARE warns that while 'the material is firmly based on Christian teaching', the course leader 'may encounter embarrassment, even hostility at first and this needs to be anticipated and worked through'.[4] Ground rules for teaching sessions should include respect, non-judgementalism, openness, trust and confidentiality. But why should CARE's teaching on sexual conduct arouse hostility among Christians?

Parents First claims that discussions around sexual language are very important. Activity 6 requires parents to categorise a list of sexual words into polite, neutral, clinical and rude/offensive. For example, the words for sex are, sleep with; making love; sexual intercourse and screwing. Other words on the activity sheet are penis, female genitalia, and oral sex. It is stressed that parents will not have to show their completed activity sheet to anyone else or share their words with the group. If the 'group is quite comfortable with sexual language, the words can be anonymously collated on to a flip chart and used to illustrate the discussion on appropriate sexual language'. The discussion that follows focuses on how the rude words make them feel, 'the importance of working out what type of language children should use' and 'the importance of parents and children being familiar with sexual language other than the "proper" word, to avoid innocent mistakes'.[5] Apparently CARE believes that it is important for Christians to have a vocabulary of lewd words, but why does this information need to be collated anonymously? Is it because the offensive words might

---

Parents First

Activity 6

SEXUAL LANGUAGE

	'Polite' word/ inoffensive	Neutral / inoffensive	Clinical	Rude / Offensive
Female genitalia				
Penis				
Sex	Sleep with	Making love	Sexual intercourse	Screwing
Oral sex				

Parents First – Sex education within the home
CARE – Course Leader's Manual

arouse a sense of shame? Most Christians know that the Bible warns us to avoid obscene language (Ephesians 5:4).

Activity 11 is designed 'to help parents gain confidence to talk to their children about sexuality'. Parents are given a starter card and invited to share their experience or ideas about the subject.[6] On the back of each card are suggestions to help guide discussion. Below are two examples. Notice the amoral nature of CARE's guidance and the absence of biblical instruction. There is no advice that parents should warn their children to flee the evil desires of youth (2 Timothy 2:22).

CARE's new sex education programme, *Evaluate... informing choice*, launched in October 2003, aims to bring a fresh, modern and direct edge to sex and relationship education. CARE's vision is that its new programme should be available to every school in the UK. At the core of *Evaluate* lies the belief that every young person is unique and capable of making healthy choices. CARE believes 'that many issues confronting young people stem from low self-esteem... '[7] This appeal to self-esteem is entirely in line with guidance from the Department for Education, which emphasises the importance of building self-esteem in

---

Discussion starter 16

Your 18-year-old wants his/her partner to be able to share his/her room at the weekends.

1   How would you feel about this?

2   What would you want to discuss:

    a)   Their sexual relationship?

    b)   Their intentions?

    c)   Contraception?

    d)   Nothing - it wouldn't happen?

    e)   Levels of trust?

    f)   Temptation?

Discussion starter 15

Your daughter of 15 says she wants to go on the pill.

1   How would you feel?

-   Disappointed   'How could she let me down?'

-   Pleased   'I'm glad she has come to talk about it.'

2   What would you want to talk about with her:

    a)   The legal situation?
    b)   Your views?
    c)   Her feelings?
    d)   The side effects?
    e)   Her future?

3   What questions might you ask her?
4   How approachable are you as a parent?

Parents First – Sex education within the home
CARE – Course Leader's Manual

children and young people in both primary and secondary schools.[8] The problem with the appeal to self-esteem is that it ignores the moral dimension of life, persuading young people that their sexual choices can be made on the basis of how they feel about themselves and not on any objective moral standard.

The *Evaluate* programme provides advice on condom use in accordance with the policy of the World Health Organisation (WHO). The document 'Education Policy, Aims & Code of Conduct' explains CARE's position on condoms:

> As the *Evaluate* programme provides education about choices available to people in the light of HIV & AIDS and other sexually transmitted infections, this will include education about condom use. The *Evaluate* programme does not promote the exclusive use of condoms as the only choice for young people with regard to sexual behaviour. Rather, *Evaluate* educators provide such education in accordance with the World Health Organisation position, which is 'abstinence and fidelity between uninfected partners and safer sex can prevent the transmission of HIV. Safer sex includes non-penetrative sex and sex using condoms'. *Evaluate* educators do not give out condoms in schools nor are condom demonstrators part of these presentations.

While an article in CARE *Today* concedes that *Evaluate* 'is not overtly Christian', CARE claims that God is working through their sex education project. According to the *Evaluate* manager, 'God's heart aches for young people. We're confident that He is working though this project, intervening in a tragic situation.'[9] But who is this god? Who is the god who teaches that low self-esteem is the main problem facing children? Who is the god who teaches young people to use a condom consistently and correctly every time? Who is the god who propagates the policies of the World Health Organisation in the name of the Christian faith? If CARE had simply said that their sex education programme is not Christian, they would have been speaking the truth.

CARE's teaching on sexually transmitted infections (STIs) is also based on the advice of the WHO. (Note CARE prefers the term STIs rather than STDs – sexually transmitted infections rather than diseases.)

The leaflet, *Quite a Catch,* is important for it provides another example of the amoral nature of CARE's approach. According to the leaflet:

> **Anybody who is having sex can get an STI**. Nearly all STI's are on the increase. Not all are curable, but all are preventable.
>
> **What's the best option?** The World Health Organisation has stated that the best way to avoid becoming infected with an STI is to stay faithful to an uninfected partner for life.
>
> **What else?** Delaying becoming sexually active is a positive health choice. Having fewer sexual partners reduces the risk of infection. Using a condom correctly every time means that you are less likely to get an STI but it is not 100% safe. Whether you've had sex or not, you have a choice about your sexual health. It affects your whole person, not just your body. Take care of yourself.

The assumption behind the leaflet is that sexual activity among young people is inevitable so they need a few pragmatic tips for avoiding STIs.

Quite a Catch (CARE)

The statement that 'anybody who is having sex can get an STI' implies that 'unprotected sex', not sexual immorality, is the cause of STIs. So 'anybody who is having sex' needs to 'protect' themselves from diseases such as gonorrhoea, genital warts and HIV. But this is nonsense. It is only in the amoral world of sex education that 'anybody who is having sex' is at risk. In the real world, those who are faithful to their marriage partner are at no risk – they don't need to practise 'safer sex'.

Quite a Catch refers to the authority of the WHO to inform young people that 'the best way to avoid becoming infected with an STI is to stay faithful to an uninfected partner for life'. Apparently CARE, along with the WHO, sees nothing wrong in sex between an 'uninfected' couple, provided they 'promise' to remain faithful for life. The leaflet subtly insinuates into the mind of the young virgin that a 'promise' of lifelong faithfulness makes sex before marriage OK. The doctrine of the 'uninfected partner' comes from a mindset that has demoralised sexual conduct.

Quite a Catch advises that 'delaying becoming sexually active is a positive health choice'. What does it mean to delay becoming sexually active? For how long should a young person delay? A few months? A year? Until they meet a really attractive boyfriend or girlfriend? There is nothing in this advice to indicate that sexual activity outside marriage is wrong.

The most disturbing aspect of CARE's approach to sex education is that it demoralises sexual conduct. Its teaching about STIs and condoms is based on the authority of the WHO and ignores biblical truth. Like the FPA and Brook, CARE teaches children how to use condoms so that if they decide that they want to have sex they are able to practise 'safer sex'. CARE seems to be unconcerned that teaching about condoms could inflame sexual lust and may be perceived as condoning sexual immorality. CARE's position is contrary to the biblical command that among Christians there must not be even a hint of sexual immorality (Ephesians 5:3).

The difference between abstinence and chastity

One of the subtlest ways of demoralising sexual conduct is to substitute the notion of sexual abstinence for the biblical virtue of chastity. Yet many Christians are deceived into believing that abstinence is consistent with biblical morality. But this is not the case. Abstinence is a pragmatic choice to refrain from certain, unspecified sexual activities for an unspecified period. The *abstinence message is fundamentally amoral* and does not recognise the concept of sexual immorality.

An important point to grasp is that virtually all sex education programmes have their own version of 'abstinence'. Advising young people to delay the onset of sexual intercourse until they feel ready is central to sex education ideology. All sex education programmes advise those who feel they are not yet ready to say: 'No, I don't want to have sex with you now.' The essential point to understand about 'abstinence' education is that it offers young people the choice between delaying sexual activity and 'safer sex'. In other words, young people are presented with two options and invited to choose the one that makes them feel most comfortable, and whatever choice they make is right for them. Hence the advice from sex education literature, 'Remember, it's your body, your choice and your right to say no. Only have sex because you want to.' Some people are misled into believing that this message, which encourages young people to delay the onset of sexual intercourse until they are ready, is consistent with biblical morality. But this is a wrong understanding of biblical truth. Delaying the onset of sexual intercourse, or abstinence, or learning to wait until the right moment, is a pragmatic decision based on the feelings and desires of the young people involved, and has nothing to do with biblical standards of right and wrong.

Chastity is a moral decision to obey God's will in the realm of sexual conduct. It is a biblical virtue that is based on purity of the heart and mind. As a Christian doctrine, it encompasses every aspect of our life, the way we think, the way we speak, the way we act. It is a way of life that seeks after God's holiness in every aspect of conduct. There is a world of difference between abstinence and chastity. *One is based on the flawed wisdom of man, the other on the moral law of God.*

Compromise around the ABC of sex education

Probably the first person to coin the phrase ABC in the context of sex education was the Health Secretary of the Philippines, Juan Flavier. He argued that the biggest barrier to AIDS prevention was ignorance about condoms.[10] Because of the Catholic Church's opposition to contraception, he decided to combine condom promotion with the messages of abstinence and faithfulness (A for Abstain, B for Be faithful and C for use Condoms), which made it appear that the prevention strategy was consistent with the moral stance of the Church.

The ABC approach to sex education has become popular among Christian organisations. The Christian Medical Fellowship (CMF) is in the forefront of a campaign to persuade the British Government to adopt the ABC approach. According to the General Secretary of CMF, Dr Peter

Saunders, 'The Government has persistently clung to promoting condoms as the main plank of its policy to counter the highest rates of teenage STIs in Europe, when what is really needed are policies aimed at behaviour change. The best way to counter this epidemic effectively is to promote real behaviour change through such programmes as the very successful ABC (Abstain, Be faithful, Condoms) programme in Uganda or the Love for Life programme in Northern Ireland.'[11] The General Secretary of CMF claims that the ABC model is based on biblical principles.[12]

Dr Trevor Stammers, Chairman of the Public Policy Committee of CMF and a prominent Christian commentator on sex education, recognises the benefits of the ABC approach. 'Uganda's ABC programme has led to dramatic decreases in HIV infection rates for over a decade. No country in the world has seen its HIV incidence fall through condom promotion alone. Changes in primary sexual behaviour are always present when HIV rates decline. Safer sex is first about partner choice and then condom use, *but both are important*. There are valid criticisms of the ABC approach but its critics and proponents alike should work together if the Ugandan success is to be maintained and replicated in other countries.' Dr Stammers concludes, 'What the ABC success teaches is that a *range of options* is now needed in the UK to help teenagers to defer sexual intercourse until they are in a secure, committed and loving relationship; to encourage faithfulness and partner reduction among the sexually active – and to promote condom use among those who engage in higher risk sex [my italics].'[13] Is this advice based on biblical principles or the policies of the WHO?

Remarkably, CMF is also campaigning for churches to work con-structively with the Joint United Nations HIV/AIDS Programme (UNAIDS) and the WHO in tackling the global HIV crisis. In a press release CMF actually encourages churches and prayer groups to use the resources available online from the website of the UNAIDS Programme, despite the amoral nature of much of the material.[14]

Christian Aid is an equally ardent supporter of the ABC philosophy. The report *Dying to Learn* claims that good quality sex education reduces levels of pregnancy and STIs, and asserts that 'condoms, used correctly and consistently, are effective in preventing HIV infection among young people who are sexually active'.[15] While talking about sex is hard, 'it is critical that the churches, and others in contact with young people, engage with them on issues of sex and HIV, and that they support others in their efforts to do so'. Sex education needs to be 'open, frank and supportive, promoting abstinence, faithfulness and safer sex'.[16] In other words, Christian Aid is in favour of a frank version of ABC.

Oasis Esteem, the largest Christian sex education programme in England, provides resources and training for volunteers to deliver sex education in secondary schools. According to the head of Oasis Esteem their sex educators have found that the message of abstinence – 'you don't have to have sex'; 'it's okay to wait'; 'not everyone is doing it' – is actually very liberating for young people facing peer pressure to become sexually active. However, teaching young people solely about the benefits of choosing abstinence and delaying sex could never be considered complete sex education. 'With this in mind, Oasis Esteem has decided to adopt the ABC model, which teaches the benefits of sexual abstinence, be faithful to your partner and condom use for those sexually active with more than one partner. It is the approach favoured by the World Health Organisation and credited with reducing HIV/AIDS infection rates in countries like Uganda.'[17]

Many secular organisations, including Marie Stopes International (Uganda), are passionate supporters of the ABC approach. Their leaflet, *Life is precious… guard it well*, teaches the range of options that Dr Stammers believes are needed in the UK. The leaflet advises a young person, 'You still have a long life ahead of you and you will want to keep it that way. HIV/AIDS is preventable, so avoid the virus by thinking carefully before you have sex and choose from ABC.'

Why ABC?

A Abstain from sex altogether. If you don't have sex, you don't take a risk. This is the only way to ensure that you don't get HIV/AIDS and other sexually transmitted infections - It's 100% effective!

B Be faithful to one uninfected partner. If you and your partner have protected yourselves in the past, and stick with each other in the future without taking other partners, you can avoid the risk of HIV/AIDS and other sexually transmitted infections.

C - If you cannot be sure of your partner's sexual behaviour either now or in the past, and you want to have sex, then you need to use a condom.

Life is precious – Marie Stopes International (Uganda)

The leaflet explains the ABC approach as follows:

A – Abstain from sex altogether. If you don't have sex, you don't take a risk. This is the only way to ensure that you don't get HIV/AIDS and other sexually transmitted infections – it's 100% effective.

B – Be faithful to one uninfected partner. If you and your partner have protected yourselves in the past, and stick with each other in the future without taking other partners, you can avoid the risk of HIV/AIDS and other sexually transmitted infections.

C – If you cannot be sure of your partner's sexual behaviour either now or in the past, and you want to have sex, then you need to **use a condom**.

If you choose to have sex, you can avoid the risk of contracting HIV/AIDS and other sexually transmitted infections by using condoms. It's your future... make your choice.

The ABC approach to sexual conduct propagated by Marie Stopes and that advocated by CMF, Christian Aid and Oasis Esteem is one and the same. Moreover, ABC is now at the centre of the HIV/AIDS prevention strategies of the WHO and the United Nations. The WHO states that abstinence, faithfulness and condoms are among the essential components of a comprehensive prevention programme, which include 'delay of sexual initiation, abstinence, being safer by being faithful to one's partner when both partners are uninfected and consistently faithful, reducing the number of sexual partners, and correct and consistent use of condoms'.[18]

In November 2004 an article in *The Lancet*, the prestigious medical journal, signed by nearly 150 experts from around the world, including many Christian organisations, called for consensus around the ABC approach to prevention. Among those who have endorsed the article are Professor Michael Alder (adviser to the British Government on sexual health), the chief executive of the Alan Guttmacher Institute and senior officials from UNAIDS, WHO and the World Bank. The article concludes that 'the time has come to leave behind divisive polarisation and to move forward together in designing and implementing evidence-based prevention programmes to help reduce the millions of new infections occurring each year'.[19] This consensus around ABC means that Christians can now join with secular organisations in constructing and delivering sex education programmes.

The question arises whether the ABC approach is based on biblical principles, as claimed by CMF, and therefore should be promoted and supported by Christians? The answer must be a resounding no! We have seen enough to understand that ABC is fundamentally amoral. It simply provides young people with a sexual menu from which to select the option that most satisfies their sexual needs. Is CMF really asking us to believe that Marie Stopes International is propagating a programme that is based on biblical principles? The hidden agenda of ABC is to compromise the Christian witness against the evil of sex education. Those Christians seated around the ABC table have come to an accommodation with the detestable teachings of the sexual revolution. The real objective of ABC is to entice Christians to compromise their stand on biblical truth—to replace biblical teaching on chastity with a sexual menu that includes abstinence. Under the ABC umbrella secular humanists and Christians, who have abandoned biblical teaching on sexual conduct, are now working in partnership to design so-called evidence-based sex education programmes.

The threat imposed by 'Christian' sex education

Today the spirit of the mad prophet Balaam has invaded the Church. For the sake of financial gain, to please a pagan king, and because he loved the wages of unrighteousness, Balaam taught the people of God to sin by committing sexual immorality. Sex education programmes developed by 'Christian' organisations are deceiving many into following the shameful ways of the sexual revolution and bringing the way of truth into disrepute.

In my view the threat imposed by so-called 'Christian' sex education is greater than that of the secular educators. At least the secular educators are openly amoral. They are, after all, promoting a sexual revolution. We know that they are hostile to the Gospel of Christ and their opposition to the biblical view of sexual conduct is plain for all to see. The 'Christian' sex educators, on the other hand, have an appearance of respectability as they teach their 'nice' version of sex education in the name of the Christian Church. Their sex education programmes are replete with fine words such as 'abstinence', 'healthy choices', 'positive values', 'self-esteem', 'informed decision', 'delay sexual debut', but behind this facade of words is the amoral teaching of the sexual revolution.

The apostle Jude warns of certain men who have crept in unnoticed. They are godless men who change the grace of our God into a licence for immorality (Jude 4). What is so tragic is that these amoral 'Christian' sex education programmes are being funded and supported by Christian people. And worse, most churches are content with the status quo, are content to leave the moral instruction of the nation's children in the hands of these compromised organisations.

God is not pleased! Christians who would be faithful to the gospel of Christ must have the courage to speak out against the widespread false teaching that is twisting the Christian witness and misleading children and young people. The folly of the false teacher must be made plain to all. It is imperative, therefore, for Christians to oppose sex education, both secular and 'Christian', with open Bibles. The reason sex education is wrong is because it is contrary to God's word.

Endnotes

1 *Your School and Sex Education*, CARE, 1996, p3   2 Ibid.
3 *Sex and Relationship Education*, CARE for Education, 2001
4 *Parents First – Sex education within the home*, CARE, 1995, p5
5 Ibid. p35   6 Ibid. p56
7 CARE *Today*, 'Sex in the Cities', Issue 10, Spring 2006, p6
8 *Sex and Relationship Education Guidance*, DfEE, July 2000, p9, p10
9 Ibid. CARE *Today*, 'Sex in the Cities', p6
10 Glob AIDS news, Health Secretary's ABC spearheads prevention in Philippines, Larraga PS, 1993; (4): pp5–6.
11 Christian Medical Fellowship, press release, Teenage sexual health, 20 November 2005
12 *Triple Helix*, The AIDS pandemic, Peter Saunders, Winter 2004
13 TG Stammers, As easy as ABC? Primary prevention of sexually transmitted infections, editorial, *Postgraduate Medical Journal*, 2005, vol. 81, pp273–275
14 Christian Medical Fellowship, Press release, Christian Medical Fellowship says World undervalues role of Christians in Fight against HIV/AIDS, 29 November 2004
15 *Dying to learn: Young people, HIV and the churches*, A Christian Aid report, Mary Garvey, October 2003, p1
16 Ibid. p24
17 *Guardian Unlimited*, 21 September 2005, Breaking the taboo, Catriona Martin
18 WHO position statement on condoms, *Condoms and HIV Prevention* (July 2004)
19 Halperin DT et al., The time has come for common ground on preventing sexual transmission of HIV, *The Lancet*, 27 November 2004, 364, pp1913–4

7

The case against sex education

There is no doubt that sex education has failed dismally in its stated aim of reducing teenage pregnancies, sexually transmitted diseases and abortions. This is because contraception among the young has an exceptionally high failure rate. Few people realise that most teenagers who become pregnant have been using contraception. For example, a study of 147 teenagers with unplanned pregnancies found that 80 per cent claimed to have been using contraception at the time of conception.[1] Research on teenage pregnancies in general practice shows that most (over 71 per cent) who became pregnant had discussed contraception with their GP in the year before they became pregnant.[2]

When I was Director of Public Health for Croydon Health Authority, all the evidence I came across convinced me of the inability of contraception to prevent pregnancies among teenagers. To illustrate this point I examined the relationship between the use of condoms at first sexual intercourse, and the conception rate among under 16-year-olds, for the period 1975 to 1991. My letter, published in the *British Medical Journal*, showed a remarkably powerful correlation between the two trends, with *pregnancies increasing with increasing condom use* (see graph). A feasible explanation is that the promotion of contraception among the young has contributed to an increase in sexual activity, which in turn has inevitably contributed to the increase in teenage pregnancies. The letter concludes, 'Sex education and the national campaign to promote contraception through safer

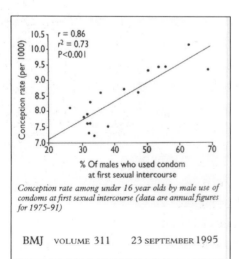

Conception rate among under 16 year olds by male use of condoms at first sexual intercourse (data are annual figures for 1975-91)

BMJ   VOLUME 311   23 SEPTEMBER 1995

sex campaigns have undoubtedly been successful in increasing the proportion of teenagers who use condoms. Most people assume that increasing the use of contraception leads to a reduction in unplanned pregnancies. Yet my analysis shows that this has not happened. A plausible explanation is that the main factor in unplanned teenage pregnancy is contraceptive failure, not the lack of contraceptive knowledge and availability.'[3]

The deception of 'safer sex'

The 'safer sex' message has deceived many children into thinking that they can become sexually active without adverse consequences, provided they have 'protected' sex with condoms. We now have a remarkable paradox – despite a nationwide campaign promoting condoms since the early 1970s the problems that sex education claimed it would solve have actually got worse. Providing children with free contraception, without the knowledge or consent of their parents, is an open invitation to engage in sexual intercourse without any apparent danger, an invitation to enjoy 'safer sex'. By removing the fear of pregnancy many young people are recruited into a promiscuous lifestyle.

Hundreds of thousands of children who have suffered the emotional trauma and moral guilt associated with sexual promiscuity, can testify to the fact that the 'safer sex' message is dishonest, cruel and misleading, for it hurts young people, especially young girls, who often feel that they have been used as a sexual object. Those girls enticed into promiscuity by the 'safer sex' message, find that they have entered not into a world of sexual fun, as promised by the sex educators, but into the dark world of sexual immorality, characterised by anxiety, insecurity and fear. Amoral sex education, of course, does not

Roll with it! (Brook)

acknowledge the existence of sexual immorality and glosses over the moral devastation that results. The unavoidable truth is that sexual immorality has consequences. Sadly, sex outside marriage has serious consequences – the worry of resorting to emergency contraception, the pain and guilt of abortion, the shame of sexually transmitted disease, the sadness of broken promises, children without fathers, to mention some of the more obvious.

The false assumptions of sex education

The edifice of sex education is built on the false assumption that it is natural for children to be sexually promiscuous. Consistent with their amoral approach, sex educators promote the idea that children are likely to have sex the moment they become sexually mature, and so the issue is simply to prevent them from becoming pregnant.

But the assumption that children are basically promiscuous is false, for human beings, created in the image of God, have a conscience that writes the law of God in their hearts. Children who have been taught the basics of biblical morality know in their conscience that it is wrong to 'have sex' for pleasure. Young girls, in particular, have a natural aversion to promiscuity, for they have an innate fear of becoming pregnant. However, it is not only the fear of pregnancy that acts as a natural restraint, but also the knowledge that to 'have sex' is a huge life-changing step, from which there is no returning. Such a decision cannot be taken lightly and in their hearts most women do not want to become sexually active before they are married. Most women know that their body is not meant for sexual immorality (1 Corinthians 6:13).

Those who ignore the warnings of their conscience feel shame and guilt. This is why children are too ashamed to let their parents know that they are getting a supply of condoms from the local clinic. This is why clinics that treat sexually transmitted diseases are clouded in secrecy. This is why young women are encouraged to hide their supply of condoms in their purse for the shame of being found out.

A second false assumption is that 'sexual ignorance' causes sexual tragedies. According to the sex educators, parents are largely to blame because they do not talk to their children about sex. This fallacy is used as a pretext for teaching children a large number of completely unnecessary sexual facts. Sex education uses these facts to introduce unnatural sexual thoughts into the minds of innocent children on the pretext of giving them the 'truth' about sex. Here it is important to make the distinction between facts and truth, for *facts are not truth*. Facts can be used, and are used, to corrupt and deprave, whereas truth always has a moral dimension and never corrupts. Truth is found in God's word and always promotes sexual morality and what is decent, pure and right; facts, on the other hand, contain no moral dimension and may be used to promote immorality. So facts about sex, without the moral implications that flow from those facts, do not constitute truth, but a pathway to sexual temptation.

How many good parents do you know who talk to their children about sex? Why do the most devoted, good parents, who really love and nurture their children, not spend time teaching them about sex? Are these parents, as suggested by sex education, failing their children? No. God has always intended that sex should be an intensely private matter between husband and wife. Indeed, the Scripture speaks of the unpresentable parts of our body that should be treated with special modesty (1 Corinthians 12:23). It is unnatural for parents to talk openly about sex with their children. This is why the thought of discussing sex with our children produces a deep sense of embarrassment. Our God-given sense of embarrassment protects us against indecency and promotes modesty. The incessant clamour that children must be 'educated' about sex comes from the teachings of Marie Stopes and the FPA, not from the Bible.

The case against sex education

The story of sex education is a story that must strike fear into the hearts of most parents. From the evidence that we have uncovered it is clear that sex education is being used as a medium for communicating the amoral ideology of the sexual revolution. The sceptre of Friedrich Nietzsche, Sigmund Freud, Marie Stopes and Alfred Kinsey lurks behind the sex education that is being foisted on to our children. And behind the revolutionaries lurks the great deceiver, the father of lies, the prince of darkness, the one who hates children with a diabolic malice that is beyond human comprehension. We have uncovered one of the devil's dark, cunning schemes. Perverted, depraved ideas are now being taught by a massive, government-funded indoctrination campaign. Slowly but surely these revolutionary ideas are taking root among our children. Slowly but surely the revolution against biblical standards is producing its inevitable fruit. As a consequence it is now commonplace for children to believe that they can do whatever appears to be right in their own eyes – that they can even set their own standards of sexual behaviour. Many are being persuaded that it is their right to make an informed decision to have sex when they want to, provided they practise 'safer sex'. Many young lives are being shattered by the consequences of sexual immorality.

Parents cannot simply abandon their children to the evil ideology of the sexual revolution that is being propagated by amoral sex education. My advice, therefore, is that parents should exercise their right to withdraw their children from sex education lessons. Even then, their children will still be exposed to 'safer sex' messages which all state secondary schools are required by law to teach. Nevertheless, if a sufficiently large number of parents take a firm stand by withdrawing their children, and explain the reasons for doing so, then the authorities will have to take notice. Parents are encouraged to teach their children the divine plan for sexual conduct, presented in the appendix.

Christians, who are the salt of the earth and the light of the world, have an obligation to take a stand against the outrage of amoral sex education. Church leaders who are true to the faith must have the courage to speak out against the systematic demoralisation of children that is taking place in state schools. Remaining silent in the face of such evil is not an option. The Church has been entrusted with the divine plan for sexual conduct and it is required by God that those who have been given a trust must prove faithful.

Endnotes

1 Pearson VAH, et al., Pregnant teenagers' knowledge and use of emergency contraception, *British Medical Journal*, 1995; 310: p1644

2 Dick Churchill et al., Consultation patterns and provision of contraception in general practice before teenage pregnancy: case control study, *British Medical Journal*, 2000; 321: pp486–9

3 Williams ES, Pregnant teenagers and contraception. Contraceptive failure may be a major factor in teenage pregnancy (letter), *British Medical Journal*, 1995; 311: p806–7

Appendix

What is the teaching that
sex education never mentions?

The divine plan for sexual conduct

Learn why the message of 'safer sex' has
failed young people

ES Williams

The divine plan for sexual conduct

This leaflet will teach you the truth about sexual behaviour. As you learn to understand the real meaning and purpose of sex, you will be free to conduct yourself in the way that God intended. You will no longer be held captive by a false teaching that seeks to undermine the traditional moral standards on which our civilisation is based. You will understand why the 'safer sex' message propagated by sex education is misleading, dishonest and cruel.

So take time to read this leaflet carefully. Keep it in a safe place and read it again and again. Think carefully about its message, for it contains divine wisdom that will change your life forever.

The sexual nature of mankind

The first thing to understand is that sex is God's idea. The God of the Bible, who created human beings in his own image, created mankind male and female. In His great wisdom God created people who would reproduce sexually. He could have chosen a non-sexual way of reproduction, but He did not do so. God had in mind a sexual relationship between a man and a woman right from the very beginning of Creation. After He had created the first man (Adam) and woman (Eve), God saw that His creation, including our sexual nature, was very good. So our sexual nature is part of God's perfect creation, one of God's greatest gifts to humanity. God's first command was 'be fruitful and multiply' (Genesis 1:28).

It is God's will that children should be born into a family created by marriage. The first marriage came about in this way. After God had created the man from the dust of the earth, He said: 'It was not good that man should be alone; I will make him a helper comparable to him' (Genesis 2:18). So God caused the man to fall into a deep sleep, and created woman from a rib taken from the side of man. This is an important truth, for it symbolises the closeness of the relationship between the sexes.

In the first marriage, God brought Eve to Adam, who was overjoyed at the sight of his wife. He cried out with delight, 'This is now bone of my bones and flesh of my flesh; she shall be called Woman because she was taken out of Man.' God ordained marriage with these words: 'Therefore a man shall leave his father and mother and be joined to his wife, and they shall become one flesh' (Genesis 2:24). The symbolism of the rib provides a picture of marriage, for at marriage the rib returns into the man, as husband and wife truly become 'one flesh'.

The purpose of our sexual nature is twofold. First, to create a permanent, 'one flesh' union between a man and a woman called marriage, the only rightful place for a sexual relationship. The second purpose is to produce children, born into the family created by marriage.

The meaning and purpose of marriage

Most people get married at sometime, so it's important to understand what the Bible teaches about marriage.

1. A man leaves his father and mother

At the heart of marriage is the idea that a man leaves the family into which he was born and forms a new family with his wife as they set up home together. The leaving of the parental family is a public event, so that everyone knows that a couple is married and intend to live together.

2. A man is united to his wife

At marriage a man is united to his wife in a lifelong union. They promise to live together as husband and wife and to be faithful to each other, whatever the circumstances, until 'death us do part'. The union of husband and wife provides the fullest expression of mutual loving companionship that humans can experience in this world.

3. No longer two, but one flesh

Jesus emphasised the one flesh union created at marriage when he said: 'So then, they are no longer two, but one flesh. Therefore what God has joined together, let not man separate' (Matthew 19:6). Jesus is saying that husband and wife are no longer two separate individuals but one unit (a new family), for husband and wife are joined together in a profound relationship that has been ordained by God.

By joining together in a sexual relationship, husband and wife have the potential to create a new life which is the natural fruit of their marriage union. And the children born into the family illustrate the concept of 'one flesh' – both parents contribute equally to the genetic make-up of their children, and the children have family traits of both parents. This is why there is a physical resemblance between children and their parents.

The husband is the head of the family; he must love his wife as he loves his own body. The wife must respect her husband and submit to him; she watches over the affairs of her household. Parents must discipline their children, and children must obey their parents (Ephesians 5:22–33).

The virtue of modesty

The divine plan has given us standards of moral conduct (virtues) to safeguard marriage, the family and children. Modesty is the virtue that reveals the inner beauty and moral strength of a woman. A woman's beauty does not come from her outward appearance but from 'the hidden person of the heart, with the incorruptible beauty of a gentle and quiet spirit, which is very precious in the sight of God' (1 Peter 3:4). The true beauty of a woman comes from her moral character.

Modesty teaches a woman to cover herself in a way that is discreet and decent, and reveals itself in the way a woman dresses, talks and behaves. A modest woman does not make a show of her sexual attributes. She is not sexually provocative. She hides her eyes from explicit images and closes her ears to explicit talk. Her conduct discourages lust and encourages faithful love. And more, modesty makes a woman attractive to the one man who chooses her to be his wife. The false teaching of 'safer sex' entices a woman to make a sexual spectacle of herself. The immodest woman is destroying her womanhood by her foolish behaviour.

The virtue of chivalry

Like modesty, chivalry is a virtue that reveals the inner moral character of a man. It is a mindset that compels a man to treat women with honour and respect, because they are the weaker partner in that they are sexually vulnerable through pregnancy, childbirth and motherhood (1 Peter 3:7).

A chivalrous man is courteous and caring towards women, and does not take sexual advantage. He learns to practise self-control and is not ruled by sexual lust. He does not treat women as sex objects, and rejects casual sex as wrong. He is prepared to keep himself sexually pure. When he gets married, he is faithful to his wife. He loves her, protects her and provides for her and for their children. So young woman, seek a chivalrous man as your marriage partner.

The danger of sexual immorality

The Bible gives the strongest possible warning against sexual immorality. 'Flee sexual immorality. Every sin that a man does is outside the body, but he who commits sexual immorality sins against his own body' (1 Corinthians 6:18).

And we know that this is true, for all around are the dreadful consequences of sexual sin. There is an epidemic of sexually transmitted diseases (STDs) among young people. Chlamydia, an STD which may cause infertility in women, is now so common that the Government has set up a national screening programme. Clearly, the message of 'safer sex' has not, as promised, protected young people from STDs. Why? Because sexual immorality is a sin against the body, and those who fall into this sin are harming their own body.

It is tragic when single young women become pregnant. Some choose to have an abortion because they see no other way out. Some choose to go ahead with the pregnancy in the knowledge that the baby is going to be born outside a proper family structure, and without the care and protection of the baby's father.

Young person, you must understand that contraception offers no protection against the ravages of sexual immorality. Even among those who manage to avoid the obvious dangers of an unwanted pregnancy or STD, they still have the problem of a bad conscience, for they know in their heart that sex outside marriage is wrong. The fleeting pleasure of illicit sex is not worth the heavy price demanded by sexual immorality.

Remember, only the Bible, God's eternal Word, provides a sure, trustworthy guide to sexual conduct. The Bible teaches that impurity, sexual immorality, homosexuality and adultery are the enemies of marriage and the family. For marriage to thrive, all forms of sexual immorality must be condemned as wrong.

Sexual purity

The Bible answers the question – how can you keep your way pure? 'By guarding it according to God's word' (Psalm 119:9). A young woman should be trained to be self-controlled and chaste (Titus 2:5). The word chaste means clean, pure, undefiled. Chastity is the virtue that comes from a pure heart and mind. A chaste woman is careful not to defile herself sexually, for she knows that sex is meant for marriage and is determined not to become sexually active before she is a married woman. She is faithful to her future husband even before they have met.

A young man who wants to keep himself sexually pure must flee the lusts and passions of the flesh (2 Timothy 2:22). Jesus said that whoever looks at a woman with lust in his eyes has committed adultery with her. So young man, avoid any situation in which you are likely to face sexual temptation. Keep away from the immoral woman. 'Do not lust after her beauty in your heart, nor let her allure you with her eyelids, for by means of a harlot a man is reduced to a crust of bread; and an adulteress will prey upon his precious life. Can a man take fire to his bosom, and his clothes not be burned?' (Proverbs 6:25–27)

Good news for young people

The divine plan, outlined above, is based in God's wisdom. The wise young person is the one who builds their house on the solid rock of God's word. The difference between the divine plan and the message of 'safer sex' is like the difference between light and darkness. 'Safer sex' is, by its very nature, an attack on the virtues of modesty, chivalry and chastity, for it does not understand the meaning of sexual purity. It never mentions marriage and it does not teach that any form of sexual conduct is wrong. Instead, it encourages young people to do what they want, even to negotiate 'safer sex' with a partner.

The good news of the Christian gospel is that it offers forgiveness from all sin, including sexual sin, to those who truly repent and turn to Christ for salvation. Young person, place your trust in the wisdom of the Bible, for it is the only sure guide to sexual conduct. God's plan for sexual conduct is the right way, and is good for men, women and children.

Written by ES Williams
Scripture from the New King James Version of the HOLY BIBLE
Freely available from Belmont House Publishing

Other publications by Dr ES Williams

Other publications by ES Williams

The Great Divorce Controversy

This book examines the divorce issue from the widest possible perspective, searching for the ideas and attitudes that underlie the move to mass divorce. The history of divorce in England and America is described and evidence shows the effect of divorce on men, women and children. Biblical teaching as it relates to marriage and divorce is outlined. A major factor in the move to mass divorce has been the changing view of marriage that flowed from the Reformation, which emphasised the secular nature of marriage and permitted divorce for adultery and desertion among other things. The author concludes that the Christian Church needs to re-examine its teaching of marriage and divorce in the light of biblical truth.

Belmont House Publishing. Hard cover, pages 416, illustrations 22, index.
ISBN: 0 9529939 3 7

Lessons in Depravity – sex education and the sexual revolution

This book is a devastating critique of sex education ideology. The history of sex education in the UK is outlined. As the story unfolds so the link between the explicit messages of the sex educators and the ideology of the sexual revolution become increasingly clear. In view of the inherent moral dangers, parents cannot afford to stand back and leave the moral instruction of their children in the hands of State sex education.

Belmont House Publishing. Soft cover, 328 pages, 6 illustrations, index
ISBN: 0 9529939 5 3

What is going on in Christian Crisis Pregnancy Counselling?

This book examines the nondirective, options crisis pregnancy counselling provided by CARE's network of counselling centres and shows how it is no different from that provided by pro-abortion counselling services. The underlying philosophy of CARE's approach is based on situation ethics rather than biblical truth.

Wakeman Trust and Belmont House Publishing. Soft cover, 91 pages
ISBN: 1 870855 45 0

Cohabitation or marriage?

This booklet discusses the increasing trend in cohabitation in the UK. It teaches the biblical view of marriage and shows why cohabitation is not a good idea. The negative consequences for those who choose to cohabit is demonstrated. The authors show that marriage is God's intended way, and conclude that cohabitation is morally indefensible.

Authors: Rev Declan Flanagan and Dr ES Williams

Belmont House Publishing. 28-page A4 booklet

ISBN 0 9529939 0 2

Sex education, sexual immorality and the Bible

This booklet explains to young people what sex education is really about. Examples from sex education literature demonstrate its amoral ideology. The 'safer sex' message is shown to be false and misleading. The Bible is quoted to warn of the dangers and deceptiveness of sexual immorality. The booklet shows why sex is meant for marriage, and explains the virtue of self-control.

Belmont House Publishing. A6, 24-page booklet

ISBN: 0 9529939 4 5

Sexual conduct – advice for young men
Sexual conduct – advice for young women

These companion booklets contrast the sexual advice provided by the wisdom of the world, with the wisdom of God's word. Sexual conduct is placed in a biblical, moral context. Marriage and the virtues of sexual purity, modesty and self-control are explained. The booklet for young women stresses the importance of modesty and for young men the virtue of chivalry.

Belmont House Publishing. A6, 32-page booklets

ISBN: 0 9529939 6 1 (Young women). ISBN: 0 9529939 8 8 (Young men)

Differences between the teachings of Sex Education and The Bible

This leaflet describes the ten essential differences between the amoral ideology of sex education and biblical truth.

A5, 4-page leaflet

Essential differences between Marriage and Cohabitation
Describes the biblical view of marriage and the arguments against cohabitation, with evidence of its harmful effects.
A5, 4-page leaflet

The divine plan for sexual conduct
This leaflet provides young people with a biblical account of God's plan for sexual conduct. It describes the biblical view of marriage and the virtues of purity, modesty and chivalry.
Three-fold A4 leaflet

A critique of Christian Aid's report – Dying to Learn: young people, HIV and the churches.
The Christian Aid report encourages the Church in Africa to teach young people the ABC approach to sexual conduct. This critique demonstrates the amoral nature of this approach. The biblical view of sexual conduct is promoted.
Produced by Belmont House Publishing. A5 pamphlet, 12 pages

The above mentioned leaflets are available from Belmont House Publishing free of charge, or they can be downloaded from:
www.belmonthouse.co.uk